DO YOU THINK THIS IS ALL THERE REALLY IS?

MONICA MARTIN

BALBOA.PRESS
A DIVISION OF HAY HOUSE

Copyright © 2021 Monica Martin.

All rights reserved. No part of this book may be used or reproduced by any means, graphic, electronic, or mechanical, including photocopying, recording, taping or by any information storage retrieval system without the written permission of the author except in the case of brief quotations embodied in critical articles and reviews.

Balboa Press books may be ordered through booksellers or by contacting:

Balboa Press
A Division of Hay House
1663 Liberty Drive
Bloomington, IN 47403
www.balboapress.com
844-682-1282

Because of the dynamic nature of the Internet, any web addresses or links contained in this book may have changed since publication and may no longer be valid. The views expressed in this work are solely those of the author and do not necessarily reflect the views of the publisher, and the publisher hereby disclaims any responsibility for them.

The author of this book does not dispense medical advice or prescribe the use of any technique as a form of treatment for physical, emotional, or medical problems without the advice of a physician, either directly or indirectly. The intent of the author is only to offer information of a general nature to help you in your quest for emotional and spiritual well-being. In the event you use any of the information in this book for yourself, which is your constitutional right, the author and the publisher assume no responsibility for your actions.

Any people depicted in stock imagery provided by Getty Images are models, and such images are being used for illustrative purposes only. Certain stock imagery © Getty Images.

Scriptures taken from the New King James Version. Copyright © 1982 by Thomas Nelson, Inc. Used by permission. All rights reserved.

THE HOLY BIBLE, NEW INTERNATIONAL VERSION®, NIV® Copyright © 1973, 1978, 1984, 2011 by Biblica, Inc.® Used by permission. All rights reserved worldwide.

The ESV® Bible (The Holy Bible, English Standard Version®). ESV® Text Edition: 2016. Copyright © 2001 by Crossway, a publishing ministry of Good News Publishers. The ESV® text has been reproduced in cooperation with and by permission of Good News Publishers. Unauthorized reproduction of this publication is prohibited. All rights reserved.

Print information available on the last page.

ISBN: 978-1-9822-6795-7 (sc)
ISBN: 978-1-9822-6796-4 (hc)
ISBN: 978-1-9822-6794-0 (e)

Library of Congress Control Number: 2021908307

Balboa Press rev. date: 05/05/2021

For me.

CONTENTS

Preface ix
Tune In—Listen to the Universe Talk xvii
Send Me a Sign xix
"Thank you for Your Assistance!" xxi
Worship xxiii
Acknowledgments xxix

DREAMS

Chapter 1   The Dream 1
Chapter 2   Never Lose Your Sense of Wonder 7
Chapter 3   The Need Is Great 12
Chapter 4   Leap of Faith 15

SIGNS

Chapter 5   He Goes before Us..25
Chapter 6   Living the Life 33
Chapter 7   Man in the Mirror 38
Chapter 8   "How" Is the Magic! 41
Chapter 9   The Promise 44
Chapter 10   All We Have Is Now 50
Chapter 11   The Covenant 58
Chapter 12   True Love 67

VISIONS

Chapter 13 Trust Yourself 73

WONDERS

Chapter 14 Forgiveness 85
Chapter 15 Blessings Come in Disguise 92
Chapter 16 Angels among Us..97
Chapter 17 Knowledge and Understanding..................................100
Chapter 18 California Dreaming 103
Chapter 19 Reset...109
Chapter 20 You Are Enough! 112
Chapter 21 Always Honor Your Inner Voice................................ 118
Chapter 22 Grounded 124
Chapter 23 Dreams Do Come True..127

PREFACE

I have been hiding. But it is *now time*! Time to remove the veil.

This book is a personal account of my experience with the omniscient presence—the God of the universe. I believe he makes his presence known through *all* of creation. The question is not, "Is he real?" but rather, "Are we paying attention?"

He speaks to us through *dreams, visions, signs,* and *wonders*.

Some call this happenstance, irony, or coincidence. For me, it is evidence that we are not alone. Even the very breath we breathe, we did not ask for, nor can we control it.

As I write these words, my daughter, Karly, is currently experiencing a mysterious respiratory issue that is literally taking her breath away. We have sought out various doctors and specialists in an effort to get to the bottom of this. She coughs and gasps for air. It is heartbreaking. I have been crying a lot. I feel helpless that I cannot give her breath or breathe for her.

Our breath is not a resource we can purchase at a store. It is, however, the *life force* energy that allows us to experience the amazing gift of life. It is also the fact that proves that we are not living life on our own. This breath we breathe is freely given.

A few nights ago, I too lost my breath. I was struggling to breathe. I was gasping for air. In those moments, I thought, *this may be my last. What if it is?* For years, I've been telling myself, when I am ready, I will share my story. But how will I know when I am ready? What if I die today? How would my story be shared?

Everybody dies, but not everybody lives.

> The graveyard is the richest place on earth because it is here that you will find all the hopes and dreams that were never fulfilled, the books that were never written, the songs that were never sung, the inventions that were never shared, the cures that were never discovered all because someone was too afraid to take that first step, keep with the problem or determined to carry out their dream.
> —Les Brown

> Don't die with the music still inside.
> —Dr. Wayne Dyer

Listen to your intuitive inner voice and find which passions stir your soul.

Telling these stories does just that for me! When I have the opportunity to share them is when I feel the most alive.

There are many reasons why one decides to write a book. I have a story to tell—one of hope, perseverance, and, above all, love. So many things happen in a day—a chance meeting, encouraging words spoken at just the right time, trials and triumphs changing everything in the blink of an eye, all of it there for our personal growth and spiritual development. The human spirit is amazing. When unleashed, it can do incredible things!

I have spent the last thirty-plus years trying to find God. When I was a young girl, I asked to go to church. Why? Because I heard that was where I would find him. I tried many different belief systems, searching for which best suited me, yet I still felt incomplete and lost within each one. There was always a set of rules to follow and a way of being in order to be accepted and complete. On my quest to become this approved person, I began to question everything.

In the scriptures it is said, "By this all will know that you are My disciples, if you have love for one another." (John 13:35) (NKJV).

Love. What is love? It is said that God is love. But what is love? And where do I find this God I seek?

"Ask and you shall receive." "Seek and you will find." "Knock and the door will be opened." "Be still and know that I am that I am."

I tried it all, or had I? I was always on this quest to seek him, to find him in temples and churches. Through this quest, I discovered the importance of stillness.

Be still, and know that I am God. (Psalm 46:10) NIV

So, I tried to do just that. Sit. Do not think. Meditate. It was such a difficult concept for me because I always felt the need to understand him in my head rather than within the stillness. I had to learn to bring my awareness to the nothingness, the space between all that is. When you do, you will see it is the space between that makes all things, that defines all and gives all meaning.

Through this process, I've come to learn that there is a clear difference between believing and knowing.

- ♦ *Believing* means you have chosen a truth, but *knowing* means you are certain about that truth.
- ♦ *Believing* always leaves room for doubt, but *knowing* leads to confidence.

- ♦ *Believing* is a blind trust, while *knowing* is trusting with awareness.

Knowing is an inner awareness, not a belief. A belief must be explained and defended, but when you "know that you know that you know," you become aware of a universal intelligence inside all living things, which allows it to be. It is this essence that gives us life and breath, circulates our cells, and forms our very existence. It is from this space that we see. It is what gives and takes away life.

Still, I did not fully understand. It left me questioning.

> Love your neighbor as yourself.
> —Matthew 22:39 NIV

Do good works, for "faith without works is dead" (James 2:26) NKJV.

Religion taught me to do for others, put them first: JOY—Jesus, others, you. This left me feeling empty and resentful while seeking acceptance and approval.

Notice me.

Like me.

Choose me.

The focus was on me and doing what I needed to do in order to be found worthy in his eyes.

My feelings of emptiness and resentment led me to understand that I needed to adjust the lens.

> Rather than being your thoughts and
> emotions, be the awareness behind them.
> —Eckhart Tolle

Go Within

You were created on purpose, for a purpose. The love of oneself is the guiding principle to understanding *who and what* you are here for. So many of us wander the world wondering what it is all about, missing the signs and wonders sent forth from our creator. I am here to share my journey to God with you, including my struggles and understanding.

For so long, I wanted to know who and what this God was and is.

You are not of your own creation; your very breath is proof of this. There is an inner intelligence, a voice that calls us all. Your imagination is a gift. Nothing is without it. Dreams and passions are placed on our hearts for a purpose. They drive us to learn more, consuming us. Our souls are deep, longing exploration. We will never know all there is to know, but I have come to learn that we are loved and supported all throughout the journey. Even on days when we think we are all alone, that no one knows what we are going through, a miracle happens.

> Miracles don't happen to you. They happen through you.
> —Mary Davis

mir·a·cle

noun

1. a surprising and welcome event that is not explicable by natural or scientific laws and is therefore considered to be the work of a divine agency.

    Oxford Languages

Example: Just then the phone rings. It's a friend you haven't talked with in a long time, letting you know you've been on their heart and they are reaching out to see how you are doing. Right on time. *How did they know?* It was that longing, that passion, that drive in their soul to call and check in, and on the end of the receiver, there is a *knowing* that someone is looking out for you. Even in our darkest hour, he is there.

Something similar happened while writing this book.

I woke up to this text message on September 9, 2020, sent at 6:45 a.m., from my friend Tonya, whom I had not spoken to in over a year:

"Here's a morning affirmation that I have to share! Everything is working to my advantage. Something wonderful is happening for me now. My world is taking care of me. Everything is going according to plan. Things are working out perfectly and will continue to do so with ease."

I responded, "I appreciate that! I have been struggling with believing in my dreams lately, and this is perfect. Thank you!" I continued to share with her some of my recent struggles and told her that I have been working on my book, but with every passing day, I was becoming more discouraged due to the time it was taking. I have always had an issue with time. It felt like it was taking too long! I was becoming doubtful in myself and my ability to complete it. I struggled with my worth being tied to doing rather than being.

Her response, "OK seriously, I woke up to use the bathroom last night and heard the affirmations telling me, 'You are worthy of good things. You deserve the best life has to offer,' telling me to hug that little child that did not feel that as a kid. It was such an overwhelming feeling of love for myself that I had not had in a very long time."

I responded, "Wow! That is beautiful. Why did you choose me to send it to?"

She wrote back, "Praise God! Yes! Push through, Monica! You chose it to be heard, Monica! I sent it to a few friends, and your name popped up! Like attracts like. We have more control over our minds than we want to believe!"

"I love you and thank you!" I responded. Her text could not have come at a more perfect time.

During my journey, I have found there is a persistent theme within our existence; we are constantly trying to understand the wonders of the universe. Generation upon generation, we all want to know the meaning of life. Somewhere along the journey, we get lost in the confusion of the inner workings of the system, going through the motions of life rather than living and thriving. We are almost robotic in a sense. We spend most of our adult lives climbing the ladder, working hard to buy the car, the house with the picket fence, complete with a dog in the yard. We get married, have children, and are left longing for more. *What's missing*? You can't quite figure it out. It's like a checklist shows up in your head:

- ✓ Career
- ✓ Marriage
- ✓ Home
- ✓ Children

All the boxes are checked, but what's it all for? You begin to question everything. Unhappiness and displeasure settle in where accomplishment and pride once resided.

You start to get hobbies and collect stuff. You begin to work harder to buy the next big something. Even that is not enough. In time, you begin to realize it is not some*thing* you desire but rather some*one*. That someone is you! The lack of purpose, the lack of passion has left you without *you*.

> Where there is no vision the people will perish.
> —Proverbs 29:18 (NKJV)

Some of us happen upon an epiphany, an aha moment, and a life course change of direction happens. Others of us are left searching for happiness in the *things* of our lives. We feel unfulfilled and might go so far as to seek professional help in navigating these feelings. Newsflash! There is nothing wrong with you. It is just that the universe is trying to get your attention. Can you relate to any of this?

Dr. Wayne Dyer refers to these as quantum moments. He references a study in the movie:

The Shift

For the men, the *morning* of their focus is on:	And in the *afternoon*, it switches to:
1. Wealth, the accumulation of money	1. Spirituality
2. Sense of adventure	2. Personal peace
3. Achievement	3. Family
4. Pleasure	4. God's will
5. Respected	5. Honesty
For the women, the *morning* of their focus is on:	And in the *afternoon*, it switches to:
1. Family	1. Independence
2. Career	2. Self-esteem
3. Fitting in	3. Spirituality
4. Attractiveness	4. Happiness
5. Self-esteem	5. Forgiveness

Quantum moments are so vivid and intense that they are forever embedded within our souls. When they come, they are unexpected, uninvited, and unforeseen, resulting in personal transformation, pushing us into a greater awareness of ourselves and what is most important.

This definitely explains what has happened to me.

TUNE IN—LISTEN TO THE UNIVERSE TALK

Life speaks to us all the time. It comes in the form of whispers, nudges, and kicks. Whispers are subtle occurrences that plant seeds of doubt. These whispers are the tiny voices in the back of your mind that ask, *Do I really want to take this promotion? I won't be able to go to my son's soccer game or my make it to my daughter's recital. I worked so hard to get here, but now I'm not so sure it was worth it.* The nudge is a reminder of the voice in your head questioning your decisions, creating obstacles, making it difficult to hold onto the idea that the life you are living is the one you truly want. On your way to work, the first day of your newly promoted job, you get pulled over and get hit with three citations. Is that the universe nudging you, keeping the whispers alive inside your head? Then there is the undeniable kick. These kicks seem to come one after another, almost making your decisions for you. For the last six months, you have heard the whispers, felt the nudges, and still cannot decide if this new job is what is best for you, causing your performance to lack its previous shine. It is noticeable to you and to others around you. Suddenly, the universe comes in with a sweeping kick, and you lose your promotion and your job. At first, you might feel an overwhelming feeling like your life is out of control, but really, this is the way the universe talks to us. It's not loud, and it's not obnoxious; it's soft and subtle.

Each time I have gone into the silence and tuned in to the language of the universe, the whispers, nudges, and kicks have shown me the way.

SEND ME A SIGN

Sometimes the universe's subtlety can be easily overlooked. The signs it gives us might not grab our attention as directly as a whisper, nudge, or kick. It could be finding a coin along your path that seems to have been perfectly placed. For some reason, the coin brings you a sense of peace. Or having a complete stranger say something to you that you did not even know you needed to hear. Have you ever seen the same time or number over and over again? You just can't seem to get away from it. *Is there something to this?* Yes, I believe there is!

This universal Spirit is not out there somewhere; it is in everything and everyone, all around us, and therefore is intertwined in the ordinary moments of life. The universe expresses itself in great simplicity and knows your needs before you know your needs. All you have to do is trust you are being guided and supported and be on the lookout for signs. There is a divine order and timing to everything. Trust in the synchronicities of life. Pay attention to the signs. Persistence and repetition are a surefire way to tell if the universe is trying to tell you something:

Our bodies talk to us through the language of aches and pains, signaling us that we are out of alignment; our thoughts and feelings are creating dis-ease in the body. Our dreams send us messages, guidance, and answers. This means is often used to connect with those who are leading super busy lives. It is the only time we slow down and the universe can catch us. It may contact us through people. This may happen through meeting a chance encounter; someone happens to tell you something or does something that sparks something within or triggers a deep knowing inside of you. It could be getting a text or a phone call from someone, hearing a message on the radio, or overhearing a conversation. Animals speak; whenever they cross your path, they are coming by to share a message. Objects do too; for example, when you find something you've been looking for or when an object falls off the shelf or out of a cabinet, triggering something from the past, supporting a new idea, or proving to be the answer you were seeking. Certain numbers being repeating may have a hidden meaning. I refer to these as angel numbers. You just happen to look up at the clock, and it is 3:33, and it seems to shout out to you.

As I put together this piece, the time on the clock seemed to shout out to me 3:33 p.m., so I looked up the message from the angels.

Angel Number 333—JoAnne Scribes

> Tells you that the Ascended Masters are near you. They have responded to your prayers and wish to help and assist you in your endeavors and with serving your life purpose and soul mission.

"THANK YOU FOR YOUR ASSISTANCE!"

Have you ever had a random song pop in your head or a certain song come on the radio, and it seemed to speak to your soul? When these things are random and you feel a connection to the song you hear, it is probably something you should explore. Pay attention to the lyrics, as there may be a message for you. Random thought pops into your head out of nowhere. It may be a solution to a problem or something you feel inspired to do. Pay attention and see what it might mean for you. Words or pictures may be trying to tell you a message. It may be on a billboard, Instagram post, or in a magazine; for whatever reason, the words seem to shout out at you—a deep feeling of knowing this is the right thing to do, or you feel something is off. You hear something or read something that resonates with you, and you don't know why, but it does. This is your inner truth being awakened. There is a deep truth within us all that is connected to the universal truth, and when you hear this truth, it seems to awaken something deep within your soul. Pay attention to it and follow it, for it knows the way!

Malfunctions of technical devises and glitches in the system may be occurring to distract you or stop you—protecting you from making the wrong decision. Setbacks, roadblocks, and delays may all be ways that the universe protects you. These things are usually out of your control. It is best not to resist but to accept it as a sign. Everything seems to be falling apart. This is a great opportunity to rethink and reevaluate our lives. Same can be said when everything seems to be aligning and flowing; you feel inspired, you're in the zone, and opportunities seem to fall right into your lap. You are manifesting your desires and feeling connected.

Life is pretty incredible when you take the time to tune in. It will take you on a magical journey if you are willing to move.

I have spoken with countless others who have shared that there comes a time when you start to question things you've done, questioning all you thought you were supposed to do. Then you arrive and think, *do you think this is all there really is?*

WORSHIP

We invest our time and our money in watching sports, attending concerts, and other forms of entertainment. We admire the athletes, singers, and actors who get to live out their dreams. Muhammad Ali, Katy Perry, Jim Carrey ... you get the picture. They believe in themselves and their abilities. They are not trying to be anyone or anything other than who they are, and that is what I believe we truly admire. We all have this greatness inside. It is the human spirit. Trust it. Go deep within to find it. You will then see all that you need is already there. We are fully equipped to be who we were created to be. We tend to worship other humans who are alive, those who seem to be superhuman. We look at them in awe and pay to witness their magnificence.

Side note: Something to keep in mind—you cannot see something in someone else that does not already exist in you.

The truth is all of us are created with seeds of greatness inside of us. In order to tap into this greatness, you must defy the limits placed on you by those outside of yourself, people who tell you that you can't, you aren't, and you won't.

Keep in mind that a limit is there because it was the last place someone else reached, not because it is the top. *Anything* is possible if you believe it to be! Stop being confined when you were made to soar! We long for this freedom, but how do we achieve it? We do so by becoming fully expressed. No reservations. No regrets. We act upon the longing of our hearts, accessing our inner child. Somewhere deep inside, you know what that is.

You finally muster up the courage to grab hold of it, but then doubt creeps in, and the questions begin. *Who am I to go against what they have told me about myself?*

Who are you? You are an amazing, magical being made of stardust. You have so many gifts to open, just like those we admire and study. They know who they are.

The question is, Do you?

Answer: "Who are you not to?"

Journey to Self

I have been on a personal journey to discover who I am and what I am here for. I have adopted conventional belief systems in order to fit a mold in an effort to obtain a specific outcome, but in reality, it is only a copy—a duplicate—when I was made to be an original, one of a kind.

Just like you!

No one in all of creation will ever be you! You are unique and priceless; even your very fingerprints can never ever be replicated. More than seven billion humans occupy the earth, coming and going year after year, yet *no one* will ever be *you*. That is absolutely amazing! Awe inspiring, really. Don't you think?

Yet we spend our lives trying to be someone when we already *are* someone.

We strive for perfection and are paralyzed with fear that we are not enough. The world has taught us that we are not enough! It preys on our insecurities, self-doubt, and perceived inadequacies, telling us that if we want x, then we must be y.

> Maybe she's born with it, Maybe it's Maybelline.
> —Maybelline

That's just not true. No one and no*thing* can define us. We are ever changing. Our bodies, minds, and spirits are always evolving. We are constantly a new creation, a perfect creation in each moment of our existence.

Every seven years, our bodies go through a regeneration of every cell, yet we focus on trying to keep things the same. Think of all the fad diets and the focus on youth. The truth of the matter is, in a lifetime, we will wear many different bodies, varying in shapes and sizes. All the while, the you, the true *you*—your essence—just is.

Some refer to this as the x factor. The x factor is that stamp that God gave that is uniquely you. Think of a friend; think of everything they are and everything they are not. You cannot fully explain what makes them so special, but there is something about them, an x factor that draws you to them. That, my friend, is them, and that is you. It is where *we*, the ever-changing us, live. It is not tangible—you cannot reach out and touch it—but it is there. We know it's there.

How do we know it's there? Intuition.

Intuition

Intuition is the ability to know something without any proof. It is sometimes known as a gut feeling, instinct, or sixth sense. It is the guiding force that comes from within us, that still, small voice whispering universal truths. It is your intuition that guides you along your path. It is that spiritual knowing that bubbles up inside of each of us and gives us chills when we are most connected to our source—God.

The universe is designed to care for and guide all of its creatures, Birds have an internal compass; dolphins, bats, and whales all have sonar to navigate their world; and we have our intuition. When we know how to use our intuition, our antennae, our sixth sense, we learn how to tune in and allow ourselves to be led by the spirit within.

My Hope

I hope that you will look back on your own personal journey.

I hope these stories I share will give you a new perspective on life.

I hope that you have the courage to follow your inner voice.

I hope you trust in your calling despite what the world may say.

I hope that you listen to the ridiculous requests being made of you.

I hope to help you recall all the times you thought you were alone or lost and see that he was with you all along.

You are never alone.

Monica

Truth be told, within the *ridiculous* is where I tend to find him.

P.S. It is where I have moved in faith and seen the magic unfold.

ACKNOWLEDGMENTS

Thank you, Jesus, for showing me the way!

David Martin, thank you for answering the call and being my rock, lover, and soul mate. I love you with all of my heart! Now and forever! You believed in me when I could not. Without your support, this book would not have been possible.

Karly Martin, thank you for coming and being my angel baby. I admire your creativity and enthusiasm for life. You are my greatest teacher. I love you!

Ruff, thank you for always being there to snuggle and love on! You have licked my tears and have taught me love. There must be a reason why *dog* spelled backward is *God*. You truly are my very best fur friend.

Grandma Sarah, thank you for loving me, believing in me, and helping me to become who God created me to be. I know you are my guiding light, my guardian angel.

Diane Hubbard, my forever friend. God gave me you thirty years ago. We have been through so much together and apart. Thank you for believing in me and your willingness to assist in editing and helping to bring my vision to life! I love you!

Debbie Marks, thank you for always being there for me. You have been my greatest cheerleader and very best friend.

Dawn Bean, I love you so much! Thank you for believing in me.

Joe Lopez, thank you for the gift of forgiveness.

I would also like to thank all of my mentors, those who were brave enough to step out and become who God created them to be, setting an example and empowering me to follow my own dreams and see them through. Thank you for your words that summarize the tale I tell: Louise Hay, Napoleon Hill, Dr. Wayne Dyer, Les Brown, Michael Jackson, Oprah Winfrey, Terri Savelle Foy, Tony Robbins, Rachel Hollis, Joel Osteen, Francis Chan, Lao Tzu, Jay Shetty, Sandi Krakowski, and Joyce Meyer.

Thank you to my friends and family who have been perfectly placed throughout my journey to help me find my way: Frank Marks, Nancy Marks, Cecilia Smelser, David Reini, Kelli Thompson, Crosswinds Church, Tonya Parrott, Katie Purdy, Robert Piekos, Michelle Clark, Michelle Pitt, Tom Typinski, Trudy Sanchez, Kayla Jock, Ken and Kathy Schultz, Julie Quinn, Nate Phippen, Vince Pusateri, Mike Hardy, Brook Sager, Paige Priester, Brittany Priester, Brittany Martin, and Sheryl Murphy.

Thank you from the bottom of my heart!

DREAMS

CHAPTER 1

THE DREAM

> Sometimes you have to take a leap of faith and allow yourself to be guided by something bigger than you.
> —Anonymous

In 2009, I was having the time of my life. I was at the top of my game. People were losing jobs left and right, and I was excelling. Then I had the dream that would forever change my life. I had a dream that I was going to have a baby girl named Karly. It was beautiful. I was holding her in my arms and saw her little face and looked up and read her name written on the wall:

K-A-R-L-Y

I heard God speak to me and say, "Take a leap of faith, quit your job, put me first, and I will bless you with a baby girl named Karly."

It was incredible! I woke up and could not shake the dream. I wanted so badly to have a child, but the doctors had told me that there was no way in the world that would be possible unless I did hormone therapy treatments. Then I had this dream where God spoke to me and told me to take a leap of faith and quit my job? Ridiculous!

At first, I did not think anything more about it. After all, the very notion of it was nonsense; it was just a dream. *Or was it?* I had lunch plans with a few friends at a local wine bistro in our downtown. I told them about the dream. My friend Katie told me that she felt it was prophetic and shared with me how there are numerous accounts in the Bible, but I started to reason, *Well, that was in the Bible. Surely that doesn't happen in our time.*

A few days later, I was at church, sitting in the newly formed library with my friend Krissy, checking out the purple shelves she had just painted. In walked a woman I had never seen before. She sat down next to us at the table, reached out for my hands, laid hers upon mine, and said, "Take a leap of faith". I quickly pulled my hands back. I was in shock. *How did she know?* I did not know this woman. I had never seen her in my life. She introduced herself. "My name is Michelle." She then began to explain how she had been watching me for weeks and felt a tug to share that message with me, but because she had been fearful of how I'd react, she stopped herself. This time she needed to tell me. She said, "It is time."

Krissy and I looked at each other in amazement, and tears began to well up in my eyes. I asked her to tell me whatever else she knew. She said, "That's all I knew to tell you. I know nothing else." I could not believe this was happening. *How did she know?* I hurried off to the bathroom to fix my face. The sermon was about to begin. On my way there, I was stopped by another friend in the hallway. Her name was also Michelle, and she began to tell me how she had dreamt last night that I was pregnant and told me how she had been praying for me and that God would make a way. She felt this was a sign. At the time, I was serving as the assistant children's ministry leader. I poured my heart and soul into that space, making it as comfortable and inviting for the children as possible. I fully furnished the childcare room with age-appropriate equipment. I loved helping out with the children. It brought me much joy. I had to hurry off to the classroom. The sermon was about to begin.

Do you believe this? I was like, *For real? Is this really happening? Two people in the same day, minutes apart, confirming what God spoke to my heart in my dream.* I had to snap back to reality. This was all crazy talk. I told myself, *Stop. Stop this nonsense right now*! After all, my dreams were coming true. Right? I had just been promoted to district manager. My team was in the lead to win the incentive trip to Mexico. Life was good!

As I sat down in the classroom with the children, I could not help but replay the events that had just occurred. I was so confused. I told myself over and over it was impossible. The doctors told me there was no way. My body was not equipped to carry a child, and I had accepted that. Actually, if I am honest, part of me was a bit relieved, especially because selfishly I was having the time of my life. I had a job most people envied. I got to sell liquor for a living, attend launch parties for amazing brands, and get paid to do it! It was like an adult playground that I got to play in all day. Oh, did I mention the trips that I could win and the experiences? That year, I won the Mexico trip and two more incentive trips, one to a distillery in Kentucky and the other a relaxing week in Myrtle Beach. It truly was amazing! Why would I ever want to give this up? To do so would be ridiculous.

That was when it began—*whispers* my heart ached. I longed for that moment I had in my dream of holding that little girl, looking down at her beautiful face. Quickly, I tried to silence my mind by thinking about how it was impossible. *Think about what the doctors told you, coupled with the special gifting you had when you worked with young children.* I used to be a preschool teacher and owned my own daycare. (Ironically, my degree is in early childhood growth and development.) My nickname was the "Baby Whisperer." It seemed as though I understood their every need without them saying a word.

I reasoned with myself, *God knew I would not be able to have children, and that is why I have this special gift.* For ten years, I was able to bless and care for so many little children, each as if my own. I would then think about the dream, the lady at the church who told me to take a leap of faith, and my friend Michelle who spoke of a dream she had that I was pregnant. I started to think about the scripture about testing him to see if his Word indeed is true and how we would see signs and have visions. But due to my previous religious background, I thought I was playing with the devil. What if I was wrong? What if it was just a dream? *What if I throw this all away for nothing? What then?* Not to mention the world was experiencing the Great Recession. People were losing their jobs, and God was asking me to leave mine? That's ridiculous! I was lucky to even have one.

Can you recall a similar situation in your life where there was a series of coincidental or ironic scenes playing out, each lining up to get your attention, confirming something that had been placed on your heart?

Have you ever had a dream that seemed so real and came true?

Or have you ever received any messages in a dream?

I shared this story with hundreds of people, and I was astounded to hear how many others had similar stories to share regarding how God gave them the name of their child or told them that they too would become pregnant, or they had dreams about their yet unborn child as well.

One of the stories that stood out was from Tom. He was a friend of my stepmother's. She had put the two of us in contact. Tom was a videographer. I had recently started a cookie company and needed some publicity. He offered his services to help get the word out. During one of the visits, we got to talking about how I gave birth to the idea for yumbitz, and I shared the story of the dream that God placed on my heart. I told him all about seeing Karly in my dream and the directive that had been given to quit my job. He smiled ear to ear and began telling the tale of how he heard from God.

Tom explained, "I was an avid dreamer, recording and analyzing them for years since my youth. So, when I learned we were to have my first child, I was watching to see what our firstborn might be, boy or girl. I had always been a very spiritual person as well, something my own mother instilled with seeing the world on more levels than the naked eye allowed. 'Dreams were from God. Pay attention. It's all important.' So, somewhere in the first trimester, with everyone else guessing and pondering this new addition, I had a dream of my son. I knew it was to be a boy, that I would choose to name him Thomas John, like me. In this dream, I am on a long stairway, circular, rising to an upper level of a beautiful white mansion. The walls are bare as I begin, but as I climb each stair, letters come from out of the walls like wallpaper and then become more and more clear, in many fonts, various sizes, all in a beautiful metallic blue and floating around and past me as I stop to gaze at them. The letters are all TJ, just like that, falling and flying and in a dance around me like confetti or butterflies. And in the dream, I instantly knew the baby would be a boy and I would call him TJ. Thomas John II turned thirty-seven on May 31, 2020.

"The second dream of my second son was a bit different. We had no names chosen. We were hoping for a girl just to balance the family out, and my wife's father had passed early in her term, so many complications followed with her in and out of the hospital numerous times, from the third month on. I just wanted to make sure she and the baby stayed healthy because both were constantly monitored throughout the pregnancy. I was caring for son number one and my wife, trying to stay positive throughout for all of our sakes. Needless to say, many prayers and tears were given in this period. We were all very concerned and stressed.

In the dream, I heard childish laughing, joyous, like only kids can do. But at first, I didn't see anything except a couch in our living room. Suddenly, my son, TJ, popped his head up from behind the couch. He was giggling and looking back over his shoulder. I heard more laughing, but it was not coming from TJ. He flipped over the back of the couch, and around the corner came another boy, smaller, younger, chasing him, catching him, laughing and giggling as TJ jumped up on all sides of the couch to send the other child into uproarious laughter and glee. The two continued this chase over and around the couch, laughing and oblivious to anything else going on around them, totally in this loving, laughing, brotherly moment. I knew then that we would have a second boy, healthy in every way and a companion for his older brother for life. It honestly helped me through the tough months ahead with weekly hospital stays, where I assured my wife and son that Mom and baby would be OK. "I saw it in my dream" was my mantra.

CHAPTER 2

NEVER LOSE YOUR SENSE OF WONDER

> Always be on the lookout for the presence of wonder.
> —E. B. White

I just finished watching Disney's *Moana* at the theatre. The movie had me in tears, especially the scene of Moana singing "How Far I'll Go":

> I know everybody on this island
> has a role on this island
> So maybe I can roll with mine
> I can lead with pride, I can make us strong
> I'll be satisfied if I play along
> But the voice inside sings a different song[1]

It seemed to speak right to my heart. Oh, how my heart longed to live by the ocean. I had only been there a handful of times. Yet my soul felt like it was home. None of my friends and family could understand why I felt so connected to it. It had never been my home before. Some

---

[1] Lyrics by Lin-Manuel Miranda.

of them took offense and felt that I was too good for them, but the truth was there was this call, this pull on my heart to explore and discover where I truly belonged.

That night, I had a dream, and Grandma Cecilia came to visit me. I was walking through what appeared to be the airport food court. As I rounded the corner, I saw Grandma Cecilia and Aunt Evie sitting there. I was a little uncomfortable about running into her. I was embarrassed because I did not go to her funeral. Mind you, she died in November 2004.

I had just moved to Chicago from Detroit the month prior and recently started a new position as the director of a KinderCare. I had responsibilities to tend to, and out of fear of losing my role, I chose not to go. I was hoping she did not notice me. She called out to me, "Monica!" I looked in her direction timidly. She was so happy to see me. She had the biggest smile on her face, grinning from ear to ear. She said, "I know. It's OK. I forgive you." She shared with me how she understood why I did not go to her funeral. That brought peace to my soul. I let my guard down and smiled. My grandma and her sister were all dressed up in their Sunday best, getting ready for another trip. I told her how I always admired her traveling the world. (That is something I remember from my childhood, her sending postcards and returning with trinkets and treasures from her trips.)

She gave me a big hug. She was always a really good hugger. I told her how I had always wished to explore the world like she did and live near the ocean. She shared with me how our family was made up of big dreamers, always up for an adventure. Somehow, I felt as though she came through to grant me permission. Later that same year, my husband received an amazing opportunity to relocate our family to the West Coast.

California Dreaming!

I had written the request in my gratitude journal. With praise and thanksgiving, I made my petitions known.

> November 15, 2016
>
> Thank you for LA. I cannot wait to get there and sell yumbitz and live among the mountains and visit the ocean. We need rest and relaxation in our lives. San Diego here we come!

(We now live exactly halfway between LA and San Diego in a town called Aliso Viejo.)

Finding Dimes

We recently moved into a new home and found a dime in every room of the house. Even when we redid the basement, there were two Dutch coins found in the wall, the equivalent of ten cents. I called my friend Kelli to tell her about the dimes I kept finding. I had to tell someone!

I had just finished vacuuming the living room. I went back in to admire the work I had done and saw something shiny on the floor. It was a dime. In the office, I found a dime on one of the shelves. I found a dime in the lip of the washing machine door. I found a dime under a rag in the kitchen sink.

I was finding more and more dimes. I even found one perfectly situated on top of my clothes, in my suitcase, after I got home from a recent trip to a Joyce Meyer conference. (Crazy to think that the bag had gone through airport handling and the car ride and was then rolled into the house—and the dime never moved!)

Everywhere I looked, I kept finding dimes. I started to think I was going crazy, seeing things. Whenever I find myself feeling this way, I reach out to my friend, who always seem to understand me and the supernatural occurrences that happen in my life. Kelli is my girl! We met at Sullivan's steakhouse in Naperville, Illinois. She and I were on assignment to put together a fireside chat. When we first met, neither of us really had an appreciation for the other. Neither of us were happy we were being forced to work together. I recall walking in the restaurant with a chip on my shoulder. Right off the bat, things were a mess! Nothing seemed to be going as planned. It got so bad that I felt like I had to speak to whoever was in charge, but after chatting with Kelli for a little over a half hour, we discovered the root of the problem was someone else entirely. When I look back, it's clear that the universe allowed that issue to come up, forcing us to work together, providing a space for us to connect. After that, she became instrumental in the discovery of my intuition. She has helped me nurture the gifts that are inherent in me. She has been a blessing in my life, and I could not be more grateful for the obstacle that brought us together.

Back on track. I knew there had to be something to these dimes. I seemed to be constantly encountering them. She told me there absolutely was, and the universe had a message for me. She told me how I could ask for the person who had been leaving them to come forth and reveal themselves. So, I decided to give it a go. I had nothing to lose. Before I headed off to bed, I asked for the angels to reveal to me who had been leaving me dimes throughout the house.

That night, I had a vivid dream. I recall walking into a dark room, and as I entered, the desk lamp turned on. It was a metal lamp with a pull chain. I could make out that it was sitting on an old tanker desk.

My eyes followed the sounds that were coming from a transistor radio next to the lamp. I could see that someone was sitting at the desk. I could not see their whole face due to the shadow cast by the light. I could only make out their chin and mouth.

As they began to speak, their voice sounded very familiar. The scene became clearer and clearer … the desk, the lamp, and the radio. It was my uncle Dave (he died in 2008). "It is me that has been leaving you the dimes," he said with a laugh. "I Love a Rainy Night" by Eddi Rabbitt. His last name was Reini. He used to sing those words to me and my cousins every Friday night when our families got together for "pinnacle pants," a.k.a. card night. It was one of the coolest dreams I ever had!

When I woke up, I called my cousin Ed, his son, to tell him of the good news. "Your dad reached out to me in a dream!" I explained that I kept finding dimes everywhere and that his dad came to me in a dream and told me he had been leaving them for me.

Ed told me that he and his family had been finding dimes too! It made him so happy to hear it was his dad. They had been collecting the dimes in a mason jar for years. It was filled to the top!

Each time I thought about reaching out to Joyce Meyer to tell her what happened at her conference, I found a dime. I took it as a nudge to go ahead and do it!

When I was looking for clarification and direction for the cookie company I had on my heart to launch, I had a dream where I recall hearing this message: "You are 'Baking hopes and dreams one morsel at a time. Just believe!' I thought, *Man, that's good. That is really good stuff!* as I hurried to grab a pen and paper to jot it down before it faded away.

CHAPTER 3

THE NEED IS GREAT

Your purpose in life is a life of purpose.
—Robert Byrne

Our church's softball team found out about a local food pantry that needed volunteers to assemble and distribute Thanksgiving baskets. Guess who they chose? Me. They volunteered me without even asking. I was so mad! I did not have time for it. I had more important things to do! What? I did not know. The people pleaser in me reluctantly agreed. It was a ministry that was part of a Catholic church located in downtown Plainfield (I was not Catholic; at the time, I belonged to a Protestant church). When I arrived, I spoke with one of the volunteers who was directing traffic and explained how I was there to help. He said, "OK," then ushered me off to the parking lot across the street from the pantry and told me that someone would be by soon to give me further direction. So, I parked my car behind the pickup truck I saw in the parking lot and sat there waiting for an attendant.

About a half hour went by, and still no one had given me direction as to what I was going to do or how I was going to help. I was starting to get really frustrated! So, I got out of my car and walked over to the pickup truck. When I approached the window, a middle-aged woman rolled it down. I began to complain, "Are you upset like I'm upset? I mean, really! They ask us to come and help and leave us in the parking lot *forever*—with no direction. There are so many other things I could be doing right now. How disrespectful of them! Really! We are volunteering our time, not even getting paid for this. Come on now!"

She listened to me rant and then replied, "I don't know what you are talking about. I am in the receiving line."

I just stood there dumbfounded. *The receiving line? Well, that cannot be right. I told the guy when I got here that I was here to help. He puts me in the receiving line? Now I am so angry!*

I ran across the street toward the food pantry. The volunteers tried to stop me and ask questions. They thought I was bypassing the system in an effort to get help. No! I just wanted to get in and talk to whoever was in charge and express my anger! I wanted them to know they were wasting my time and tell them to put me to work. Finally, I found someone. I started explaining to them how I was obviously ushered into the wrong area and how I was there to help. I told them, "Put me to work."

They said, "I am sorry, but we don't need you. We are all set."

In my anger, I replied, "You have got to be kidding me. Really? You are all set? You ask for volunteers, and now you are all set?" Ridiculous! This was unbelievable. As I walked back to my car, I took note of all the cars around me. The parking lot was filled, and there was a line wrapped in and out of the lot and down the street. I thought, *all these people need assistance? In my own backyard? No! This cannot be!* I knew that hunger existed in third world countries, but not in my own backyard. I looked at the lot again and saw a sea of faces still waiting their turn. I got in my car, backed up, pulled out of the parking lot like a bat out of hell, and just cried and cried!

> Open the eyes of my heart, Lord. I want to see you.
> —Based on Ephesians 1:18–19 NIV

Have you ever been stuck in your own world, only to have the reality of things revealed to you so abruptly, harshly, and unexpectantly—changing your perspective entirely? You thought you were there for one reason, but the universe had something else entirely in mind.

That is what happened to me.

CHAPTER 4

LEAP OF FAITH

> If you risk nothing, then you risk everything.
> —Geena Davis

Fast forward seven months from the day I had the dream about my baby girl. It was Friday, October 16, 2009, Boss's Day. I decided to finally do it! I put in my two-week notice. I was trusting in God's promise to me that he'd bring me my Karly.

I had been volunteering at another local food pantry, Green Harvest, helping out as their business development manager. I was determined to connect the community to the needs of the working poor. I went door-to-door to local businesses, informing them that we existed and that we could use their help. I spent my time putting together *fun*draisers and was able to bring additional funds and resources to the pantry. All the while, I was patiently waiting for a positive pee stick. I confidently shared my story with others. I vividly recall working in the stock area with Trudy, another volunteer I had just met. I told her about how God spoke to me through the dream, and she then told me how her daughter's name was Carly but with a *c*. Coincidence? I think not. Looking back, I believe God was confirming that indeed it was he who spoke to me in the dream. *Whispers.*

However, my faith quickly turned to doubt. It was difficult to meet new people. I felt judged. They'd ask me what I did for a living, and I would reply, "I am waiting on God to bless me with a baby girl." I'd eagerly share my story with them, and they would look at me funny. They had no idea what to say or how to react. So, I surrendered it to God and began praying fervently for days … weeks … months.

Then I met a stranger, and she recommended that I seek out a holistic practitioner. A holistic practitioner is someone who takes into consideration the whole person, including physical, mental, and spiritual aspects, while treating a health condition or promoting wellness. Her suggestion made me really uncomfortable. *What in the world is a holistic practitioner? And how is that going to help me?* It felt weird to entertain the thought of seeing someone like that. But I was desperate! So, I did the only thing I knew how to do. I prayed. Then I turned to the yellow pages, randomly flipping through them, stopping on the exact page where I found a holistic chiropractor. Mind you, I had never been to a chiropractor before and was actually terrified of them crippling me. But my desperation made me open to the possibilities. I called the number and was greeted by Dave. He happened to be a chiropractor that specialized in sports medicine. I explained to him what I was looking for, and he directed me to another doctor in the area. Ironically, the office was less than a mile from my home. I called and made an appointment right away. When I went to meet Dr. R., I was filled with an intense feeling of hope. He shared with me how powerful our feelings are and what affect they can have on the body. He introduced me to the book *Feelings Buried Alive Never Die* by Karol K. Truman.

He gave me his personal copy to read and told me some steps I could take in order to get aligned for a blessing. We talked about my past, and I shed a lot of heartache and tears. I poured it all out (a whole box of tissues worth). He told me that it was necessary for the healing process. We got further that day than all my previous years working with a counselor. What a wonderful, caring person. I trusted him and began to see him regularly. He could tell that I was estrogen heavy, and after reviewing my feedback from a Specialized Health Appraisal and Nutritional Questionnaire, coupled with NRT (nutritional response testing), he was able to identify that my adrenal system had shut down and, that I was deficient in progesterone. NRT is an amazing test that uses arm strength to analyze the body's reflex points, which correlate with the organ functions that control performance, health, healing, and recovery—fascinating stuff. If you've never done this, I highly recommend it.

He then aligned me and taught me how to care for my whole self—body, mind, and spirit. He encouraged me to begin meditating, exercising, and eating right. I did just that! Each morning, I would meditate, choose healthy foods, and make it a point to get out for a walk or a jog. In the process, I made a friend out of my neighbor Sheryl. We would meet, pray together, and then go for a run. While we were running, we would both shout; "We are believing for this baby girl!" Over time, I managed to drop twenty pounds. I no longer used the word *lose*, because there is power in our words, and if you've lost something, the universe has a way of helping you find what was lost, and I had no intention of finding those twenty pounds.

About three months after I made the changes, a friend from church asked me if I was pregnant. I said, "No, I don't think so. Why?"

He said, "Because you are glowing. Every time my wife was pregnant, she had that same glow." *Could it be?* Was I pregnant? That night, I left church and hurried off to unwrap one of the Clearblue easy pregnancy tests I had under the bathroom sink. A friend of mine had gifted them to me. I took one every few hours, and every single one of them read, "Pregnant." I went through the entire box—four tests. I remember calling my husband, David, to tell him that I was pregnant; he was away on a business trip. We were overjoyed! Finally!

Although the tests said I was pregnant, I wanted to know for sure. So, I made an appointment for an ultrasound, and yes indeed, it was confirmed. I was pregnant! They said I was ten weeks along. I could not wait for the nineteenth week when we'd find out the sex of the baby.

Friday, October 1, 2010, we went in for another ultrasound. I was so nervous. I remember lying down on the table and hearing the heartbeat. Tears streamed down my face. I was watching the movement on the monitor. It was amazing. Then the ultrasound tech asked if we wanted to know if it was a boy or a girl. And we replied, "Yes!"

She said, "Congratulations. It's a girl!" I was covered in chills. Yay! Amazing! God's promise was coming true. That night, I called everyone I knew to tell them the news!

Monday, October 4, 2010, we were called back to the hospital. They needed to talk with us about the results from the ultrasound. I remember sitting on the bed in the room, waiting for the doctor. She walked in and started off congratulating us on our little girl. I was smiling ear to ear. I was so happy. It was really happening. She asked, "Do you have a name picked out?" I eagerly shared with her, "Yes! Karly." She paused, walked over to the door, and shut it. My heart sank. She then told us that she needed to bring something to our attention. Those dreadful words came out of her mouth, and I could not believe what I was hearing! She took a deep breath and told us she saw a cyst on the baby's brain, and that it could be an indicator that our little girl had an extra chromosome, called trisomy 18. I had never heard of such a thing. This extra chromosome may cause our baby's organs to develop in an abnormal way. She'd either be born with Edwards syndrome or Down syndrome. I immediately began to cry. I had just heard the most amazing news, that I was going to have a baby girl, just like God promised in the dream. And now this? The doctor began to explain that it was not too late; we still had options. *Options? Abortion? To end her life?*

She explained to us, "Babies with Edwards syndrome will grow slowly in the womb and will have low birthweight, along with a number of other serious medical problems. Of those that survive to birth, around half will die within two weeks, and only around one in every five will live at least three months. Around one in every twelve babies born with Edwards syndrome survive beyond one year, and they live with severe physical and mental disabilities. Some children do survive to early adulthood, but this is very rare." She then left the room so David and I could decide what we were going to do. To me, there was no decision to be made; we were going to have this baby however God was going to bring her into the world. She was his gift to us. So, when the doctor returned, we told her that we decided we were going to have her. She said, "OK," and told us we could check out and go home.

I was crushed. I could not help crying, and then all the questions flooded in. *Why? Why me? What did I do wrong?* It was hard to breathe. The depression was crippling. I locked myself in our bedroom closet (this was a safe place for me—something I had done since I was a small child, whenever situations became too difficult). Like a bad dream, I wanted this to go away and not be true. This went on for weeks until our second ultrasound.

November 1, 2010. Finally, the day had come. I was so nervous. The tech came in the room and told me she was going to perform the ultrasound, and the specialist would be in to take a look from there. She had me lie down on the table and began the procedure. I heard her little heartbeat. Tears streamed down my face. Oh, how I prayed for Karly's health and wholeness. The tech started laughing and commenting how it looked like she was pointing at us, as if she was saying, "Why are you getting my mom all upset? I'm fine." Moments later, in walked the specialist, saying, "Mom, I really don't know why you are here. Your baby is perfect." He began to explain how he had been studying the development of the prenatal brain since the eighties and had seen cysts like this one dissipate over time. "This is what I think will happen in your case. She is going to be just fine."

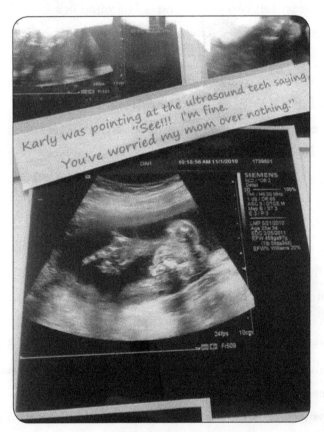

Ultrasound picture

I was beginning to realize that the universe was sending me messages by way of dreams, and I began to pay closer attention to them. They were bringing me peace, clarity, and guidance.

My Grandma Sarah came to me in a dream the night she passed.

I remember taking off my apron and shaking off the remainder of the cookie crumbs, when I was startled by a tap on my shoulder and a familiar voice saying, "Why are you crying?"

I turned around and saw what looked like a forty-year-old Grandma Sarah. I asked, "Grandma Sarah, is that you?"

She replied, "Yes."

"But you died. I'm crying because you died."

She said, "Don't be sad. I am happy! I am in the arms of Jesus." And she began to sing a hymn I had never heard before. She had so much joy in her eyes. She was truly happy. She was singing and dancing and swaying along with me, and then I woke up.

I had this peace come over my spirit. I was headed over to meet up with my family. I shared the experience I had with my dad and my aunt Marie. My aunt said that her mother sang that song a lot to them when they were growing up. She was very familiar with the hymn. It was an old Catholic hymn, "Safe in the Arms of Jesus." "Safe in the arms of Jesus, safe on his gentle breast. There by his love over shaded, sweetly my soul shall rest." My Grandma Sarah always loved singing. We are blessed to still have a few videos of her singing. The sound of her voice always brought me comfort and peace. This time was no different.

Prior to writing this book, I was a consultant for a wellness brand. I was calling on weight loss clinics. I felt like I was helping people, but over time, it became really hard for me to listen to our clients' stories without crying. I realized the issues they were facing were not really about their weight but about something much deeper, self-love. This awareness reminded me of my calling to write this book and share stories with others.

One of the owners reached out to me when she heard the news that I was leaving the company. When I told her why, she had a mouthful to share.

She texted me: "Wow! That's so awesome! I have had two dreams about my dad since his passing. The most recent dream, he was sitting on our barstool, but the stools were on the opposite side of where they actually are in our house. I was so excited to see him, and I was acting so excited, and his smile was huge, like he just knew he made my day. I placed my hand in his, and it slid through, if you know what I mean, and I looked back, and then he was gone. It still gave me such peace though. The other odd thing is just about two weeks after he passed, I was staying with my mom and was asleep. I woke up to the light on my phone, and it said I had a notification, and when I pressed it, there was a picture of my mom and dad standing on their old porch, waving at me. This picture was taken the last night at my childhood house before they moved into their condo; it kind of scared me so, I closed it and thought, *I will look at that in the morning.* The next morning, there was no notification like that. It was so strange, but that same night at my house, my son, husband, and daughter all heard a bouncing ball. My son was very freaked out, and when our daughter said, 'What if that is Papaw?' my youngest said, 'If it is, he better Stop! It's freaking me out!' Then it did it one more time, and I could totally see my dad smiling and getting a little chuckle out of that. My dad and I both heard things in our old house, and we would sometimes talk about it. Crazy! I haven't had anything recently except for the dimes I found last weekend."

Hearing that validated my own experiences. It brought me a happiness and a sense of peace to know that I was not the only person who received messages in their dreams.

SIGNS

CHAPTER 5

HE GOES BEFORE US

> He goes before us, guides us and lives inside us.
> —Monica D. Martin

I did my homework and had it all planned out. I researched everything there was to know about childbirth. I took prenatal Pilates and hypnobirthing classes. I was determined to do it right. Through my studies, I learned of waterbirth.

I began watching videos of other families who had chosen this child-birthing method and saw the joy in their eyes as they were able to experience this together as a family. Not long thereafter, I learned of midwives who were in the next town over. I went online to read all about them and to check their reviews. I liked what I saw, so I decided to set up an appointment.

I remember walking into the office and thinking, *how cool, everything is all coming together*. Although I was further along than the mothers they usually added (twenty-six weeks), we decided to move forward.

I felt like the pressure was off because the midwives would come to me rather than us trying to hurry off to the hospital, which seemed like a better idea, especially since my husband traveled for a living. It all just made sense to do it this way.

Kayla, the teenage neighbor who lived in the home behind ours, was pregnant at the same time. Her due date was the month after mine. We shared stories about our doctor visits and our plans for our babies with each other. Kayla told me how she mentioned our birthing plan to her ob-gyn and the doctor expressed concern for us. She was not a fan of home waterbirths, especially for the first birth. She asked Kayla to keep her informed as my days progressed. Kayla said her doctor also told her that she did not know how or why, but she felt she may need to help. Weeks seemed to fly by leading up to the final day, which dragged on for what seemed like an eternity. Then, my water broke. It was 4:15 a.m. on February 22 (side note: my niece Paige's birthday, and she did not want to share a birthday).

David was sound asleep upstairs. I was so confused. I had never experienced anything like it, nor did I think I had that much liquid in me. I felt as if someone had released the plug to a cooler full of water, and it was just pouring out. I managed to get to the bathroom. However, I don't know why, but I did not think to take a seat on the toilet; rather, I stood in front of it, legs spread shoulder-width apart, just watching in amazement as my body released all that water.

When it was done, I screamed at the top of my lungs, "David, this is it! She's coming!" I frantically started searching for my phone and called everyone I knew back home in Michigan—Mom, Dad, sister, best friend Diane, my cousins—and said, "She is coming. This is it!" The contractions started to get pretty intense around 2:00 p.m., at which time I called my midwife, and she sent her assistant, Karen. It was me, Robin (my doula), Karen (midwife's assistant), and David (husband) all gathered in the kitchen.

Our original plan was to birth upstairs in our bedroom, however, the heater that was promised—yeah, that was nowhere to be found. Of course, we didn't learn of any of this until the baby was almost here.

My poor husband frantically emptied the pool that had been set up in our room, carried it downstairs, and set it up again, filling it with pots of hot water. He took out all the pots we had and filled them up with water, then placed them on the stove until they were boiling and poured them into the pool. He continued to do this till it was filled up. Mind you, it was February in Chicago, and we had tile floor in the kitchen; it was cold!

In the meantime, I lay in the bathtub upstairs in the guest room with our family dog, Ruff, stressed, by my side. He knew something was up. We weren't quite sure how to calm him down, so David brought him over to Kayla's house to stay with her family.

As the hours went by, the contractions got more and more intense. I was in so much pain. By this time, my midwife called over a massage therapist to assist and comfort me, Stephanie. I tried to apply my breathing exercises from hypnobirthing class, but nothing seemed to work. So, I asked for them to turn on the Christian music channel on the TV, and I began singing along. I asked Karen to get a Bible and start reading scriptures to me. Something did not feel right. I knew deep down in my soul that something was wrong.

The midwives had me get out of the pool and labor on the couch. I was told that they could see the baby's head. They told me to start pushing. *Oh boy! She's coming! This is finally it.* What I had been waiting for all along. I pushed and pushed with all my might, but no baby was coming. I felt disappointed and defeated.

I then crawled up the stairs to labor there, hoping stretching my body would put the baby in another position to help her move down. However, that was not working either. Nothing was working! I tried to apply some of the techniques from hypnobirthing class, but to no avail. Hours had gone by; all the while, we were trying to get my breathing more relaxed. The doula seemed concerned. I was too. I was in so much pain. While we were all in the bathroom—David, Robin, and me—the doula said, "I don't make the calls, Monica, but I am worried. I think something is wrong." I thought so too. She urged us to call it. So, David helped me back to the bed and began praying for God to intervene and give direction.

It was late in the evening on February 23. The midwife arrived and started fetal monitoring. I was becoming more and more doubtful and filled with fear. The midwife was checking our heart rates and noticed that Karly's heart rate was dropping.

I was exhausted and felt as though I was dying. They were feeding me gel packs that you give to marathon runners to sustain me. I could not handle it anymore. It had been over forty hours since my water had broken. I feared we were in danger and that they needed to take me to the hospital. I was so numb. It was so surreal.

I remember seeing the red flashing lights through the window of my bedroom and hearing the roar of the sirens as the ambulance stopped in front of our home. The EMTs ran up the stairs and began asking a series of questions while they moved me down the staircase and into the ambulance. They hooked me up to oxygen. David had to follow me in the car. The midwives did not accompany me in the ambulance. I was all alone. The drive over to the hospital seemed to last forever. I recall one of the EMS workers holding my hand and telling me that everything was going to be OK and that I was safe. I needed to hear those words, "You are safe."

When we arrived at the hospital, they wasted no time in getting me to the emergency room. The staff on duty had been called in earlier that morning. I came in a little after 11:00 p.m.

Meanwhile, friends and family were following along on Facebook. David was doing his best to keep everyone up to speed. Our pastor, Ken, expressed that he and his wife, Kathy, were very concerned when David stopped replying. We later learned Ken had an awful feeling come over him that we were in grave danger. He and his wife were prompted by the spirit and went looking for me. They had no idea where to go. However, they just decided to follow their gut.

When I arrived in the emergency room, they were standing there, as if they had been waiting for me. It was comforting to see familiar faces.

All the staff were wearing *I Love Jesus!* lanyards. The nurses began their checks. One of them freaked out, stating, "There is a blood clot in front of the baby's face, and we need to get her out of there *immediately*!" They told me that I had a high temperature and the presence of an infection; therefore, they needed to prepare me for surgery. Although all of this was going on around me, I had this amazing peace about me and in me. I no longer felt pain. I was having an out-of-body experience, watching myself … not presently experiencing any of it but rather observing.

The anesthesiologist came in and told me what he was going to do. After that, the staff came in one by one. Then the surgeon came in the room, introducing herself. "Hello, my name is Dr. T." She began explaining why they needed to perform the C-section. From that point forward, it was all a blur.

When they brought Karly over to me, I just stared and cried tears of joy. What a beautiful sight she was. Just like the little girl I had seen years ago in my dream. I still could not truly digest what had just happened. I knew where I was because they told me, but I could not believe it was now over. *That was it?*

Later, the surgeon came to check up on me. She told me when she came to the OR, she picked up the clipboard, and it read, "Home birth gone wrong, Plainfield." Sure enough, when she read the patient's name, it said, "Monica."

At the same time, I was thinking, *Dr. T. Why does that name sound familiar?* Oh yeah, I knew how I knew that name. Weeks prior, Kayla shared with me how her doctor felt about my decision to have an at-home waterbirth. Her doctor told her she did not know why, but she felt that she would have to help me in some way.

Following the birth, I suffered from postpartum depression and PTSD for many years. I battled with feelings of being angry at God. I did everything I thought there was to do. I was fully prepared and educated on the birthing process. I did all the research and planned and prepared. I did not think it was fair. I felt punished. However, God knew the outcome all along. He allowed me to move forward with my plans, all the while preparing and handpicking the staff to save our lives.

Side note: When the ambulance transported me, they passed up the local hospital and took me to the larger one in a neighboring city.

Divine intervention.

I Love Jesus! lanyard

DO YOU THINK THIS IS ALL THERE REALLY IS?

Monica and Karly (winking)

I love this picture of Karly. It seems that she is winking at the camera. "See, I am just fine!" She was perfect! My lil' angel baby.

Having had this experience, I now have the gift of peace and comfort regarding death.

> God is faithful. He will not let you be
> tempted beyond what you can bear but
> when you are tempted He will also provide
> a way out so that you can endure it.
> —1 Corinthians 10:13 (NIV)

I believe that God will only give you what you can handle, and he takes it from there. I was suffering, and he took away the pain. I was dying, and he came in and saved the day. The same holds true for anyone who is suffering. I believe he gives us the strength to fight, and when we can no longer do it on our own, he steps in. He takes away the pain. I shared this truth with my stepmother after the death of her father. He had liver cancer, and in the end days of his life, it became increasingly difficult for him to eat, and he was in so much pain. It broke her heart to watch him suffer. However, I believe God took that suffering and pain on for him, just as he had done for me and does for each of us.

Think back to a very difficult time in your life—a time you did not know how you were going to get through, but you did. Do you recall how you managed? Who was present? What feelings were you experiencing? What transpired that allowed you to weather the storm?

CHAPTER 6

LIVING THE LIFE

*The biggest adventure you can ever take
is to live the life of your dreams.*
—Oprah Winfrey

Prior to the leap of faith, my team was in the lead of the sales incentive program I mentioned earlier in the book. There were only a few more weeks left, but I believed we were going to take it. Then the sales manager announced that they were rearranging the territories. I was getting a new team. Those few months while the incentive program was going on, I managed each team in the division (totaling four). Despite the shuffling, I was not going to let anything stop me! Within a few short days, my team was again in the lead. The final numbers were in!

Drum roll please.

"And the winner of the incentive for the on-premise division is Team Martin!"

It was official. We were going to Mexico! All my hard work paid off. We did it! I was so excited. But there was outrage in the on-premise. The other managers were upset and demanded a recount. And it was settled. Team Martin indeed won. We won by one bottle. We were going to Guadalajara.

I was overjoyed and so excited. *In your face!* I have a bit of a competitive spirit, if you couldn't tell. We did it despite the opposition. Having the announcement made it official. I felt like I was on top of the world. Only three teams were selected out of the entire company between the on- and off-premise divisions, and my team was one of them—and the only one from the on-premise division. All expenses paid. We were going to enjoy the fruits of our labor.

Finally, it was really happening. I was in my glory. *Yes! This is it!* My face in the photo below says it all.

Monica—smile of satisfaction!

The first night of our trip, we headed off to Cucina 88 to celebrate. It was a restaurant tucked in an old colonial-style mansion.

It had been built in the late tenth century and was owned by a general. The entrance of the restaurant was grand. The beautiful foyer with a twenty-four-foot ceiling was just spectacular. The main dining room had an open kitchen so you could watch them prepare your meal.

Since we were VIPs, we got to dine in one of their private dining rooms, where they made our meal table side. It was so cool! The spread was divine. *My favorite! Fish and chops!* We ordered the fish and steak from the case: octopus, mahi-mahi, salmon, filet—you get the picture.

Our table had about thirty of us. It was a feast. We ordered one of everything on the menu. Every inch of the table was covered with food and drink, and I thought, *this is the life!*

I was nudged by one of the girls on my team. She asked, "Do you think this is the gluttony they talked about in the Bible?"

I stopped, put my drink down, looked at the table, scanned the room, and it started—the chatter.

"I don't like this."

"Can you get us that?"

I looked up at the waiter and saw a man for the first time, not just a waiter. His shirt was tattered and stained, and his teeth were missing. I heard an audible voice in my head say, "These are my people, and you need to do something about it." *Me? What can I do about it?* My eyes welled up with tears. I had to excuse myself. I could not allow anyone to see me cry, so I hurried off to the ladies' room and took a long, hard look at myself in the mirror. Did I like who I was seeing? Then the dream came to mind again. "Take a leap of faith!"

Was this the whisper? Was God trying to tell me something? Or was it all in my head? I put myself back together and returned to the table to join my team. It was decided. I was there to have the time of my life! However, I lost the desire to eat. I love seafood, but I could not stomach another bite, so a liquid diet it was. "Yes! Another please!"

I had been trying desperately to erase and drown out the noise in my head. It did not take long before it got to me. I was having a difficult time focusing on conversation, and the room began to spin. Thank goodness I had friends who were watching out for me and helped me get back to my hotel room safely. I managed to do so without becoming a complete embarrassment.

The next thing I knew, it was morning, and we were all gathered again for breakfast. I sat down. The same girl from my team joined me. We began talking, and she asked me, "What happened last night?"

I looked her dead in the eyes and asked her, "Do you think this is all there really is?"

I began to explain how I had everything—a beautiful house, an amazing job, an awesome husband—yet there was still this hole in my heart, a longing for more. She said, "Oh no, Monica, don't go there. We are in a third world country. This is part of their culture. It is how they live." The conversation was cut short, as we were lining up to board a bus to the distillery.

I could not take my eyes off the people going about their lives. I watched them out the window, taking note of the surroundings—the graffiti-covered buildings, the children in the streets, scrounging around and begging for food. Meanwhile, our bus was filled with sounds of laughter and song. There I sat, feeling displaced, in awe of what I was seeing. I began to wonder, *Is there more to that dream?* Looking back now, I believe this was a quantum moment that Dr. Wayne Dyer spoke of—the morning of my life transitioning to the afternoon.

Were you able to identify the whisper, the nudge, and the kick?

When we look at each situation through this lens, we are able to identify a key takeaway. We may not know when or why, but we can trust in the knowing that everything happens for a reason.

Now take a moment to look back on your own life, or think about a particularly difficult time in your life. Was the universe sending you signs, signaling to you it was time for a change?

Oftentimes, this change comes by way of a passion or desire that you once had, which sometimes dissipates. That something that once brought you joy now leaves you frustrated or, worse, has become increasingly difficult. In my case, I was receiving blessings of abundance that I created for myself, while the universe was using the same situation to lead me in another direction.

> Life is always happening for us, not to us.
> —Tony Robbins

Live in gratitude and be led by awe and wonder.

Looking back on my life, I can recall moments when I felt that people had wronged me or prolonged me. Now I see the obstacle was actually assisting me to stay the course. Oftentimes, situations present themselves, and it feels like things are against you. However, keep in mind it may be propelling you.

> Reminder: planes take off against the wind.

Conventional wisdom may lead you to believe that taking off into the wind increases resistance, slowing the plane down while forcing it to burn more fuel for energy. However, there is good reason for this. Taking off into the wind allows pilots to achieve a higher altitude in less time, with less speed, propelling them!

Use the space below to jot down your personal account that comes to mind. When were things coming against you, propelling you?

CHAPTER 7

MAN IN THE MIRROR

> Sometimes when things are falling apart
> they may actually be falling into place.
> —J. Lynn

We were all gathered for the general sales meeting. Some major announcements were about to be made regarding our company merger. As I entered the room, "The Man in the Mirror" by Michael Jackson began playing. As I listened to the lyrics, my eyes began to well up with tears, clouding my vision.

> I'm gonna make a change, for once in my life
> It's gonna feel real good, gonna make a difference
> Gonna make it right ...
>
> I see the kids in the street, with not enough to eat
> Who am I, to be blind? Pretending
> not to see their needs

When I heard the verse about the children not having enough to eat, I completely lost it. I had flashbacks of the children I saw scrounging around and begging for food on the streets in Mexico. I did not understand what was going on with me.

It had just been announced that I was getting a promotion to a key account position for the new division they just created calling on the top accounts in Chicago, and I was crying? *Isn't this what I wanted? Get a hold of yourself! People would kill for this position!*

I tend to wear my heart on my sleeve. My sales manager was starting to notice the change in me and sent another co-worker to find out what was going on. I vividly remember Vince inviting me to the Piekos room to speak in private. He asked me if everything was all right. He said that he'd been sent by Nate to see what was going on with me. I told him, "I don't know. I really don't know."

Has something similar ever happened to you, changing the trajectory of your life? Recall your feelings. Were you excited, scared, lost, or confused? Those were all the feelings I was having. I felt compelled to follow my heart. I was curious to see where quitting my job would lead me. The calling on my life at that time seemed *ridiculous*. It was unreasonable. Everyone I talked to about it did not understand. Really, who in their right mind would leave a good-paying job just because of some dream?

The call became *louder*, and I could no longer ignore it. It seemed as if the world was against me. Do you remember what I told you about things coming against you?

Although I received this amazing promotion, the drive to and from the city for the accounts assigned was two hours a day. I dreaded the drive, in bumper-to-bumper traffic. I did my best to use the time wisely, to listen to podcasts and books on CD, but my heart was beginning to tell another tale. I found myself crying on a daily basis. Whispers and nudges.

I recall pouring my heart out to my mom, and she told me, "Monica, you've got to watch yourself! You are burning the candle at both ends! You really need to stop and smell the roses!"

The following Friday morning, on the way to the office, I was pulled over and received three citations in one traffic stop. I heard the universe loud and clear. It was time. I was going to submit my two-week notice.

What dream is on your heart? Does it feel overwhelming? Do you desire the outcome but have no idea as to how to bring it about? The good news is this call has been placed on your heart by God. We are co-creators, and our job is to imagine (to use our gift of imagination) and pursue it. The *how* is God's part, where the *magic* is.

> A journey of a thousand miles
> begins with a single step.
> —Lao Tzu

Or a leap!

CHAPTER 8

"HOW" IS THE MAGIC!

> We all have magic inside us.
> —J. K. Rowling

There is magic and mystery all around us. I find it beautiful and amazing. I used to think I had to have it all planned out, to have all the answers. Now, as I reflect, I see him and how I just needed to dream, trust, and believe; the *how* is the magic!

We were made for so much more. So often, we just go through the motions of life, enduring rather than enjoying, working our lives away, waiting for the weekend. By the time the weekend comes, we are exhausted. There seems to be little to no time to do the things we want to do, or time to spend with the ones we love. Oftentimes we allow distractions to pull us off course. We seek opportunities to acquire more stuff, stuff that we are told will bring us joy and happiness. What we forget is that we are co-creators made in the image of God. God is love. Therefore, we are love. We were created to be a blessing. Using our gifts and talents is what makes us happy. The truth is that under all the masks, under all the stuff we acquire, we are joy! We are happiness! It is our true essence and our God-given right!

We are taught that we need to hustle and grind in order to have an amazing life. We are taught that we must work for everything we have. Oh, the lies. It simply is not true. Yes, that is one way, but there are other options. It is all a matter of choice. The truth is he gives it to us freely. What we really need to do is get aligned for a blessing. We could be using our God-given talents and gifts to create a life where there is no need to hustle and grind. When we stop trying so hard, when we get aligned, that is what fills our souls and brings joy and satisfaction. Our existence is a gift to the world, apart from what we do. Remember, we are co-creators; we come up with the ideas, and he takes care of the how.

Think about all the care and planning that goes into a baby shower, how we all gather together to express our love and excitement for the new bundle of joy, for the coming of a new blessing. We should be living as such, noticing all the beauty around and in ourselves. It is through this we truly thrive. Each of us is born with gifts and talents, and when we are not using them, when we deny ourselves our essence of being, that's where unhappiness and depression come from. The opposite plays true for when we are using our gifts and blessing the world; our lives become rich and magical.

As I mentioned at the beginning of the book, so often celebrities are idolized, and I believe what we truly envy is that they have found their sweet spot and are reaping the financial rewards and spiritual blessings.

We are often asked as children, "What do you want to be when you grow up?" Our teachers and caregivers all encourage us to pursue careers that will pay handsomely, rather than following our passions and the longings on our hearts. If we want what they have, then we must seek thy self, our true self—*love*. We must unmask all the characters we've created. We must confront behaviors and patterns that are preventing us from receiving our inheritance. God wants to bless each and every one of us. He wants us to enjoy the journey! Every moment of it. To savor that which brings us joy. To indulge in what gives us pleasure. To unwind, relax, and reflect. To shine as a bright light. To dream, to sparkle, to melt. The list goes on.

CHAPTER 9

THE PROMISE

> So, shall my word be that goes forth from my mouth: It shall not return to me void, but it shall accomplish what I please and it shall prosper in the thing for which I sent it.
> —Isaiah 55:11 English Standard Version

I was sharing what happened at my Grandma Sarah's wake on our way to her burial service with my husband, David.

"I found a dime!" It was in between my aunt Geri and my aunt Nancy. I saw it from across the room. As I got closer, I looked down, and it indeed was a dime. "Gram's with us!" I exclaimed as I leaned over between the two of them to pick it up. I was overjoyed! I went throughout the room, holding the dime high and telling everyone.

I said, "I know it was my gram."

My aunts asked, "How do you know?"

I said, "She's new at this. When I find the dimes, they are usually perfectly placed, in the center of the tile or table or floor or wherever. This time, the dime was a little to the left."

Again, I said, "She's new at this! An amateur." As I spoke the word *amateur*, something hit our windshield.

Windshield crack

If you look closely at the photo, you will see the ridges like the edge of a dime and a smile like that of a Cheshire Cat. Ironically, the Cheshire Cat is sometimes interpreted as a guiding spirit for Alice in Wonderland.

Side note: When we took the car to the dealer to have the windshield replaced, some error was made in the reinstallation, and as a result, we paid nothing for the repair. Coincidence? I think not.

She was smiling down on me!

Background: On September 28, 2009, David and I accepted Jesus as our Lord and Savior. The same exact day seven years later, my grandma died: September 28, 2016. For me, this was proof that indeed his promises come true, and it will be no different for the promise of the resurrection!

We will meet again!

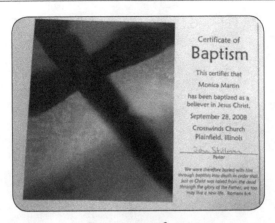

Baptism certificate

Obituary, Sarah Marks

Fast-forward to September 28, 2020. I was in the living room talking with my husband about visions I had for the relaunch of yumbitz, this time as a candy company. I was telling him about the vision of colors I had and the new names for the candies: —when I was prompted to look up a song.

My hands became extremely heavy, and I felt as if someone else was taking over and typing "Somewhere over the Rainbow" into the search bar. I was directed to click on the version from IZ. It was the first time I had ever heard this rendition.

As the song began, tears rolled down my face, and I felt as though I was getting confirmation regarding the vision I had for the dream to relaunch yumbitz, as well as my Grandma Sarah coming through for a visit.

I was always sharing with others about finding dimes. I decided to join the "finding dimes" page on Facebook. I wanted to connect with others who were experiencing this phenomenon. As I scrolled through the posts, I noticed one of the entries was from Bob, a co-worker I used to know from working at the liquor distributor. I contacted him to learn more about what he was experiencing. He shared a story with me about his son who had passed. "Mike knew that I collected coins with an emphasis on small cents. Everyone comes across an occasional penny on the ground, but for me and Liz, we were finding them very frequently after Mike passed. When we woke up on January 1, 2020, Liz found a penny on our kitchen counter near the sink. There was absolutely no reason for a penny to be there. It was dated 1979, the year Mike was born. I think Mike was telling us that we would be in for a crazy year but that he would be watching out for us.

"Another time, I feel he was looking out for me. Sometime after Mike passed, I was driving down 111th Street and drove past a place that sold headstones and statues for use in a cemetery. There was a statue of Jesus there. I was thinking of Mike and asked him, 'Who should I be taking direction from?' I then noticed that the car in front of me had one of those bumper stickers that said, 'Jesus is the way, the light, and the truth.'

God Works in Mysterious Ways

One month after Karly's first birthday, we received a card in the mail. It was from Christina, the midwife we had hired for the at-home water birth.

She outlined the payment and the remainder owed. As you will note, the slate had been wiped clean. Our responsibility—zero dollars. Coincidence? I think not! Who does that? Who just wipes away a bill like that? God! That's who!

Life Is a Blessing card

DO YOU THINK THIS IS ALL THERE REALLY IS?

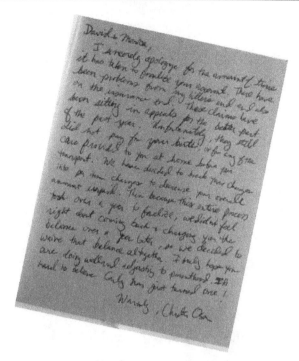

Handwritten letter from Christina

Itemized list of charges

CHAPTER 10

ALL WE HAVE IS NOW

All we have is NOW.
—Shivani Joshi

I will never forget the day I heard that audible, little voice again—my intuition, the sixth sense coming through.

I was doing dishes when I heard it say, "Go see your grandma." I always honored that little voice, but I was exhausted. We had just returned from spending the weekend in Nashville, Tennessee. We flew out there to help friends relocate to their new home.

I was so tired. I thought, *I'll ask Karly, and if she's up for going, we will.*

"Karly, do you want to go see Grandma Sarah?"

She replied, "Not today, Mommy. I'm tired. Let's go tomorrow."

I said, "Yes. We will see her tomorrow."

From that day forward, I never questioned whether or not I was hearing from God because I had just received the greatest confirmation. We did see Grandma Sarah the following day, and it was the last time.

I had been out with my sister, niece, and her friend in search of a prom dress. We were walking out of the mall, headed back to the car, when I received a frantic call from my stepmother. "Hello. Monica, your dad is on the way to the hospital with your grandma." My heart sank. It was so hard to make out what she was saying due to all the crying. I wasted no time before getting in the car and heading straight over there. Luckily, the hospital was only a mile away from the mall.

When I arrived, my family was gathered in the waiting room. I was believing for a miracle! I was not accepting it as the end. I sensed that the rest of the family had given up hope. So, I looked up the song "High Hopes." When Gram was sick in 2013, I played this song over and over for her in the hospital, and it lifted her spirits. I was hoping the same would hold true. I turned it on and turned it up and sang loudly and proudly in the waiting room.

We were invited to go see her, two at a time, in her room. So, I joined my dad. When I walked in, I saw her lifeless body lying in the bed. The machine was the only sound I heard, breathing for her. The room was cold. My grandma's boyfriend, Jim, was wailing, "Why? She is so good. She is such a good woman. Why?" I wanted to console Jim, but I couldn't. That's when it hit me. *This is it. This is the end. It is over.* My beautiful grandma was only staying alive through the machines. Her heart was beating through the pacemaker, but her breath had ceased. When I grabbed a hold of her hand, I could feel that her spirit had left, and all I was holding was this lifeless limb. My heart hurt so bad. "Go see your grandma" replayed in my head. The same little voice that spoke to me, I heard again.

It's been four years since that day, and I've never been the same. I think I left a part of my soul in that hospital room. It did not make sense to me. She had just been at my cousin Gina's wedding two weeks prior, dancing and singing with the family, and there she lay, lifeless in a cold, stale hospital room. Her hand was cold and heavy, not warm and soft as I had remembered. Less than twenty-four hours prior, she was out playing cards with her friends. I was told that she had been vomiting and suffering with a bought of diarrhea all day. She had received the flu shot less than twenty-four hours prior. Jim tried calling my dad a few times but got no answer. He then reached out to Rhonda, their neighbor and our longtime family friend, to help. She hurried over and tried to care for my grandma. However, she could not hold herself up. She kept vomiting and could not stop the diarrhea. By the time my dad got there, she was really out of sorts. They called the paramedics.

Shortly after we all made our rounds to see her, the doctors called our family into a private room. We had to decide whether or not we were going to pull the plug. They began explaining how the machines were keeping her alive.

I was crushed. But then I had to ask myself, *what did she want?*

At the wedding, my grandma told me that she was seeing red floaties, and it was becoming more and more difficult for her to make out what she was looking at. I remembered looking up what it means to see red floaties, and I could not bring myself to tell her that it could be a symptom of going blind. I remember her sharing how she wondered when her number would be up and expressing how tired she was of going to all her friends' funerals. Toward the end, she seemed to be going to a funeral at least once every month.

As much as we all selfishly wanted her to stay, she may have asked to go.

October 1, 2016, I was sitting in the White Chapel Memorial with my husband, David, and our daughter, Karly, watching the priest talk over my grandmother's casket, when I heard the same little voice inside my head say, "Now you have it. You can write your book."

I still couldn't believe it. I just could not believe she was gone. My grandma died? My light, my joy, my happiness. She was such an amazing woman. I could not believe I was sitting there. I just kept looking around. I knew it was happening. I was there experiencing it all, but it was so surreal. I guess that's why they say the first step of grief is denial. I heard that same familiar voice in my spirit say, "You will meet again. I promise! Just as I promised you your baby girl sitting beside you."

October 1, 2010, was God's first promise spoken over my life, that I would be blessed with a baby girl named Karly, and that promise came true. My five-year-old baby girl was indeed sitting next to me. To me, it was confirmation and proof that his word does not return void (Isaiah 55:11) (NKJV).

As I was walking out of the chapel, I was stopped by my second cousin, "Uncle" Ken. He told me he had something he wanted to show me. It was a video of his grandson singing "These Are a Few of My Favorite Things" from *The Sound of Music*. He pressed play: "When the dog bites, when the bee stings, when I'm feeling sad. I simply remember my favorite things, and then I don't feel so bad."

Tears started to stream down my face, and then I just began sobbing. I could barely hold myself up. I fell into his arms and just cried and cried. All the while, he was apologizing to me. I said, "No! You just gave me the greatest blessing." I began to tell him that shortly after leaving the hospital after hearing that my grandma had passed away, I was in the shower crying and hyperventilating, missing her so much. I was telling myself how I would never be able to hear her voice again, to hold her, and then I started to hear these words: "When the dog bites, when the bee stings, when I'm feeling sad. I simply remember my favorite things, and then I don't feel so bad." That song began to play in my head, and I started singing along out loud. It brought me such peace. I had not heard that song in many years. I told myself, *Pull yourself together!*

I quickly dried off, got dressed, and headed off with Karly to Meijer to shop for things that reminded me of her.

> Angel wings, Giorgio perfume, pinnacle cards,
> Aqua Net hair spray, metal hair pick, and more.

Box with mementos

"And here I am today at the memorial service, and you share this with me? I know that she is still with me!" As I was drying my eyes, I asked him, "Why did your grandson choose that song?"

He replied, "Because it is his favorite. His mother has been singing that song to him since he was born. He is now three."

After the burial, the plan was to meet up at my grandma's house. When we arrived, we were greeted by a rainbow. Remember I told you we saw the rainbow again this year?

DO YOU THINK THIS IS ALL THERE REALLY IS?

Facebook shot of rainbow—Linda Grady

A rainbow is a sign of hope and promise—the everlasting covenant between God and every living creature on earth.

So, I ask you, do you think this is all there really is? Have you received any signs or messages from the other side? Has your loved one reached out to you?

Cool Story

So, my neighbor was having a garage sale. I wandered down the street to see what kind of goodies I might find. I noticed many of her belongings were for sale. I asked her if she was planning on moving. She replied, "Yes! I'm moving to Imlay City."

"Oh, that's nice," I said. She then proceeded to tell me the story about her husband, and I was covered in chills.

She explained how he died a few years back, and she finally felt good about selling the house. I asked her if she ever sees her husband.

She was a little taken back by my asking. I asked her again, "Does he leave you signs that he is still around?"

She said, with a big smile on her face, "Yes, I think so!"

I asked, "How did he die?"

She replied, "He had stomach cancer." She started to tell me all about him and how much she loved him and how much he loved hunting—and how on the day of the funeral, the most absurd thing happened. While they were in a procession from the church to the cemetery, there happened to be a buck on Utica Road. She said that all who attended the service spoke of the buck and how he just seemed to watch everyone as they left the church parking lot. It became the talk of the luncheon. She said a peace had come over her when she saw the buck across the street.

A few years went by, and she was on the way to work at the hospital just down the street from where we lived. She was praying and talking to him, telling him how she met someone and wanted to know if it was OK for her to start dating. As she drove down our street toward my home, a buck came out from between the houses and pranced alongside her car, following her for about a half block. She couldn't believe it! It appeared to be the same buck she saw the day of her husband's funeral. She said in her heart she *knew* it was him sending her a sign. She told me how she did not share that story with too many people, for fear of how they would view her. They might think she was going crazy. But that day, she felt he told her it was OK—that he was OK and it was OK for her to move on.

I learned that the man she started dating had just proposed and asked her to move in with him, and that was why she was selling all her belongings. "Wow! What a beautiful story!" I thanked her for sharing with me. It was the first time I had ever spoken to her. Our block was long and did not have any sidewalks, so we tended to stay on the end of the block. But I am so happy I ventured down the street that day and received a gift: her story. WOW

Have you recently lost a loved one, or has a loved one tried to connect with you by sending you a sign that they are OK?

CHAPTER 11

THE COVENANT

Those who have left you are closer than you know.
—Unknown

When we were at the funeral home, my dad and my stepmother, Nancy, were asked to go back to my grandma's house to look for her mother's ring. My aunts and uncle wanted her to be buried with it. So, the two of them left the funeral home and headed over to her house to pick it up.

When they arrived, they began looking everywhere, opening up each drawer and going through each piece of jewelry in her box. Nothing. While they were searching around, a card gracefully fell to the floor and landed in front of my dad's feet. He leaned over to pick it up and read this handwritten message that caught his attention: "this is what I want on card."

Handwriting on card: "this is what I want on card"

On the flipside was a beautiful poem.

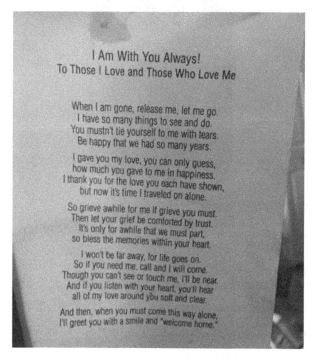

Angel poem (anonymous)

He brought it back to the funeral home and told us the story. They then asked me to read the poem at the funeral and cover the Bible reading at the mass. I happily accepted. Several family members approached me afterward and told me that when I spoke the scriptures, they were compelled to listen, and they *do not* follow the Bible. That made my heart happy!

My grandma's room

I took this picture the day before the funeral. I loved what it had to say!

As you will note, the poem was tucked in the upper-left side of the mirror. The likelihood of that falling off the mirror and onto the floor in the middle of the room, landing just in front of my dad's feet was *ridiculous* and yet another sign! "She's with us!"

My aunts decided they'd have a hundred copies made and give them to all who visited, and they threw away the original card. We all felt that Grandma Sarah was trying to tell us something.

After the burial, the death of my grandma really hit me hard. My world stopped. I lost the desire to do most everything. I felt it triggered the postpartum depression and PTSD. I went into a severe depression and felt like, *What's the point of life? Why bother?* What is the point of life if all we do is live and then die? I was angry. Why did he take her from me? I loved my grandma so much, and so did so many others. Selfishly, I wanted her to stay with me forever, but if I am honest with myself, I believe he answered her prayers by bringing her home.

On the drive home from the hospital, after they announced her death, I received a message from a friend of mine, Shawn, "Give me a call ASAP!" I called him right away and told him what had happened. He then told me about how he, too, was very angry after his father had been killed in a hit-and-run on the interstate. He could totally relate with where I was mentally and reassured me that I would heal. He then told me the reason for his call; he was reaching out to gift me a VIP ticket to the TEDx Detroit talk. I had been wanting to go, but the show was sold out on October 6 at the Fox Theatre. More than three thousand people were in attendance. I was so happy! What a gift.

TEDx tag

When the event was over, people were making their way out the front doors when I heard a trombone player playing a familiar tune. Could it be? Was it? *"These Are a Few of My Favorite Things"?* I intently tried to decipher which song he was playing, but the crowd was forcing me to move down the street, and it became more and more difficult to hear.

I was planning to meet a friend for some BBQ after the show. When she arrived, I asked her if she knew which song the trombone player was playing. She had no clue. I was deflated. I really wanted to know if what I had been hearing was truly "These Are a Few of My Favorite Things." As we finished eating, I told her my intention was to find that player and ask him. Then we heard the music playing again. I had to find him! I excused myself and hit the streets, following the tune.

I found him! He was sitting on a parking block in the street, playing.

I walked over to him, handed him some money from my purse, and thanked him for his beautiful music. He graciously said, "You're welcome." I then asked him if he had been playing at the Fox Theatre. He smiled very big and bold and replied, "Yes."

Then I asked, "What song were you playing? Was it 'These Are a Few of My Favorite Things' from *The Sound of Music*?"

He looked me in the eyes and replied, "Yes, I played it *just for you!*" His eyes twinkled, and my eyes welled up with tears. I hugged him and thanked him again. She was with me! I *knew* it. I could feel it.

I started to become very vocal about seeing signs. Whenever I found a dime or saw repeating times or numbers, I would tell my friends. It was not uncommon for them to reach out and tell me when they too found a dime or had a loved one contact them.

Here is a text message from my friend Mary:

> I was talking to my dad today (her father recently passed away) and a cardinal appeared on the tree and I found a dime in the parking lot.

Here is a text from my friend Katie following the death of her father.

> Monica, I took a walk on Monday early in the morning. I was praying and crying and at a 4-way stop and a man who had a camo hat, smoking a cigarette in a navy Ford Ranger (EXACTLY what my dad drives and wears) waved me past. I gasped because I thought it was him. I ran across the street and asked god, "why he would do that?" and I leaned over because I was crying so hard and the biggest, fuzziest caterpillar was in between my feet. I heard the word "transition" and I looked up and saw a beautiful monarch butterfly fly in front of me,

almost the entire way home. Then your flowers and note yesterday with the butterfly. Thank you for being in tune with the Holy Spirit and blessing me. Love you!

I replied, "The butterfly kisses song was in my head. I had been praying for a way to comfort you, and this was the answer I received. So, I logged onto the flower sight, and there was a 'butterfly' arrangement."

On July 26, 2020, my father-in-law died. It just so happened to be the same day his aunt had died two years prior. We all think that she came to walk him home. After his funeral, we all headed over to the family farm. It was the first time my husband, daughter, and I had ever been there. When we pulled up, we were greeted by the chickens and the peacocks. Karly was so excited! She loves animals. When she saw the peacock, she asked for a feather. Apologetically, her aunt replied, "I'm sorry, Karly. The peacocks only keep their feathers for a season, and he has already shed them all." Boy was she disappointed to hear that. Karly really wanted a feather.

She asked if it was OK to go into the coop. We said yes. She was having the time of her life in there, feeding the animals and running around playing with them. Karly tried to get her cousin Brandon to join in on the fun. He did not want to. She was not taking no for an answer, so she opened up the gate and began to pull and tug on his arm in an effort to get him to come with her. He was too scared. She gave up and went back to play with the chickens. As she opened the gate, she looked down and saw a small peacock feather. She exclaimed, "Grandpa Mike left this for me!" as she held the peacock feather up for us all to see. We were all amazed. *A feather? How did that get there?* When I opened the gate to let her in the first time, there were no feathers on the ground, only dirt and rocks. The feather was perfect. No dirt on it at all. I was in awe. Thank you, Grandpa Mike!

Karly with peacock feather

Animals Speak

Our lease was up soon on my Kia. It was time to sign on another car. We had been contemplating a different vehicle. As we pulled into the dealer lot, we were greeted by a cat. It was as though he had been awaiting our arrival; as we approached, he just sat upright like a butler at a fancy hotel greeting the incoming guests. I felt he had a message for me, so I immediately searched the internet for the spiritual meaning of a cat crossing your path. Its message: wait for your pounce.

I heard the cat loudly and clearly. I took it to confirm my gut, which said, "It is not the time. Hold off." My foot was broken anyway, so it was not the best situation to be in for test driving our next vehicle. David, on the other hand, just wanted us to pick a new car and sign before the deadline. I did not share that same sense of urgency; we still had a few days left.

A few days later, David received that text from Ernie that I shared with you before. Good thing we paid attention to the sign and we did not resign on a lease.

When Karly was five years old, she told me how she saw a dog at Papa Nanny's (my dad and stepmother's) house. She told me the story of how it was under the bed. A ball had rolled under there, and she went to reach for it when she saw a dog. She began to describe to me that the dog looked like the one from the *Lady and the Tramp* movie. So, I got my phone out and began to show her pictures of cocker spaniels. She said, "Yes, that's it! But when I went to pet it, it disappeared." Prior to marrying my dad, Nancy had a dog she named Lady, and Lady indeed looked like Lady from *Lady and the Tramp*. She had died many years before, and Karly never knew of her. A few days later, my dad called to tell me his other dog, Charlotte, had died. We believe Lady came to walk her home.

Hospice nurses report that sometimes when working with dying people they might report a vision, hallucination, or dream of someone who preceded them in death. It is often a long-lost loved one. Mothers are most common, but fathers, siblings, grandparents, and even pets frequently show up, seemingly to welcome them to whatever is next. Another thing they experience is that, even in an unconscious state, their arms will lift up as though taking someone's hand, and their mouths will move as though speaking to someone. (Published in 2014 based on interviews with patients at the Center for Hospice and Palliative Care located in Buffalo, New York.)

CHAPTER 12

TRUE LOVE

I would find you in any lifetime.
—Kanye West

Sixteen years ago, I set out on a quest to find true love. I found him! My soulmate! There he was at the B.O.B., a really cool multilevel building in Grand Rapids, Michigan, at a piano bar / steakhouse. I had decided to attend the Childcare Conference in Grand Rapids, Michigan. My plan was to expand Miss Monica's Little Friends at-home daycare to a childcare facility.

I had just asked God for a redo. I was in a religion and marriage that were suffocating me, and I wanted out! A redo! I pleaded with God and told him what I really wanted in a man. I made a checklist. I remember lying on my back on the floor in my bedroom; I was with my sister-in-law. She was my very best friend at the time. My husband and I had just gotten in another fight. That seemed to be the only form of communication we had. I started to think about all the women in my life who were married and asked myself if I thought they were truly happy and if I was headed down that same path. The answer was "No!" Little by little, the life was being sucked out of me. I was crying all the time. I no longer found joy in the little things. I could not see past the tears. I begged God for a second chance. I was telling God all the things I wanted in a man—someone who could fix things when they were broken, who could check the oil in the car, who could cook, who could clean, who could iron, who had a sense of humor, who was kind, who was personable, who was easy to get along with.

The following day was the first day of the Childcare Conference. My mom and Uncle Larry stopped by the house to see me off. I told them how Joe did not want me to go to the conference. I told them how angry he was with me. However, I really wanted to go. I felt it would be good for my career and just what I needed in order to expand my business. They encouraged me to do me. "You do you! You go because it is something *you* want to do. For you!" I did, and I met the man of my dreams, David Martin.

It was like out of a fairy tale.

I was eating dinner at this awesome steakhouse along with a dozen other women who were also there attending the early childhood conference. The food was so good, and so was the entertainment. The piano man was so fun! I love piano bars and steak. I was in heaven!

I recall two men approached our table. I was so not interested in anything they had to offer. However, a couple of the other ladies were definitely all ears. I don't know if it was because I was not giving him any attention or what, but David made his way over to me and nestled himself in between me and this other girl I happened to be sitting next to. He began to ask me, "So, what's your story?" *Story? Whatever! Get out of here!* Once I overheard him tell the others how he was a traveling businessman and was out entertaining one of his customers, I was out. I had him pegged. However, there was this little voice in my head telling me he was my soul mate. I was intrigued.

David was persistent; I'll give him that. He was not going to let me get away that fast. He began to ask me a lot of questions about me and what made me tick. I told him what I had going on in my life, and how I was on a quest to learn more about how to open up my own daycare center, and how attending this event was a stepping-stone and learning opportunity for me.

He asked to dedicate a song to me, "Tiny Dancer" by Elton John. The piano man was taking requests. He also asked to see my driver's license because he did not believe how old I was. He said I looked so young. I agreed, and he laughed. When he happened upon my ring, he began to make fun of it. He asked, "Is that a wedding ring?" I told him it was. He started laughing and said it looked like something someone would have gotten out of a Cracker Jack box. I was insulted! David continued to go on about my ring. I told him it did not matter the size; it was more about what it represented. It was enough for me.

He then invited me to join him at the dance club downstairs after we left the restaurant. I had never been to a dance club, and I *love* dancing (it's one of the things that make me feel the most alive), so I thought, *Yeah sure. Why not?* I learned that he was supposed to be some girl's birthday present. Some friends asked him to be her blind date. However, once she finally arrived, he had already made himself rather at home with me.

We closed the place down. I danced my heart out. What a super fun night! We were both sad to have the night come to an end. "Last call." They were kicking us out.

He offered to take me to the Clock Restaurant but would need to walk back to the hotel to get the keys to his truck. I joined him but stayed in the hallway. I did not know this guy. I had just met him. Going into his hotel room was a definite no-no!

We got the keys, walked out to the parking lot, and got inside the truck. He explained all the stuff in the vehicle. It was packed with a bunch of products and point-of-sale materials. At the time, he was a salesman for FUZE beverages. He had said he was there on business.

We put in our order—eggs, toast, coffee—and stayed up all night long talking. I felt like I had met my long-lost best friend. He was finishing my sentences and seemed to get me. When I got back to my room in the morning, my friend Jeanene was mad at me. She told me how worried she was when I disappeared with some random dude (back then, cell phones were not a thing like they are now). David and I have had quite the journey since our first meeting. I'll be sure to fill you in, in the next book. I'm so glad that I trusted that little voice and followed my dreams. What a ride!

VISIONS

CHAPTER 13

TRUST YOURSELF

> Trust yourself. You know more
> than you think you do.
> —Benjamin Spock

While pregnant, I headed back to Michigan for a visit. I would usually stay at my dad's, but we had a falling out, and I did not feel very welcome. The plan was to stay at a hotel—until my Aunt Marie heard and said, "I'm not having it! Stay with me! No family member of mine will be staying in a hotel." Despite my husband wanting us to stay in a hotel, I caved and took her up on the offer.

In the morning, upon awaking, she offered me some breakfast and invited me to join her in the living room for *Enjoy Everyday Life* with Joyce Meyer. I had never heard of Joyce Meyer, and at first, I was not sure I liked her. I found her to be rough around the edges. I prefer warm and fuzzy. But I watched anyway. Something about her drew me in.

Fast-forward to 2011. My husband, David, had seen a billboard while he was in town on a business trip: Joyce Meyer was coming to Pontiac, Michigan. I decided to drive to Michigan to see her. At that time, we were living in Chicago. I invited several friends to join me, but no one was available. I decided to go anyway, by myself, because it was something I really wanted to do. Mind you this was one of the first times I ever did anything on my own. My mother always said it was best to travel in pairs. It was safer. I was going regardless.

The night before the event, I met up with my best friend Diane (we have been friends since we were twelve years old). We had dinner plans to catch up. Our evening ended up in a terrible disagreement. She told me, "You've changed!" She expressed how she did not like what she was seeing and felt I had become stuck up and insulted me for driving an Escalade. The Escalade was David's choice. I just drove it there because it was spacious and I had a long drive. She kept saying that it looked *nothing* like me. She did not even know who I was anymore. We stayed up into the wee hours of morning. I was exhausted by the time I finally made it back to my hotel room. I did not feel like getting up in a few hours to drive forty-five minutes, but I did. I had made a commitment to myself.

When I arrived at the conference, the venue was packed. I thought, *Good luck finding a seat*. But the little voice in my head said, "Go up to the front." So, I made my way to the main floor. I was a few rows from the stage when a woman popped up and said, "I was saving a seat just for you!" I thought, *Really*? Her name was Suzanne. She had come alone too and told me how she felt the need to save a seat, and when I came by, she knew it was for me. Too cool. "Thank you!"

At the conference, they advertised the upcoming, Love Life Women's Conference's 30th anniversary. I had heard about it and was interested in going but was not sure how I'd get there since it was in St. Louis, Missouri, Joyce Meyer's hometown. I definitely needed a buddy to drive with. Suzanne agreed to meet me in Chicago, and we'd go from there. Two weeks leading up, she backed out, but I still wanted to go. That was when my friend Ann offered to come with me and split the room.

When we arrived at the conference, it was packed. We made our way to the first-floor balcony middle seats and sat down. The event was Thursday through Saturday. On Saturday morning, I was going to head back after the first session, but something told me to stay. I'm happy I listened.

I was so moved by what happened next that I had to share it with Joyce Meyer. It only took me a year to follow that whisper. I finally got out of my own way and removed the seeds of doubt I had planted.

It truly was a celebration of hope!

Dear Joyce Meyer

As I felt called to do so, I started writing this letter right after attending your Love Life Women's Conference—30th Anniversary.

Quickly thereafter, I started to talk myself out of it. I reasoned, *why would Joyce want to hear about what happened to me? I am just one of many millions.* However, I kept hearing that little voice in my head telling me to write you. Of late, it is getting louder and louder, happening more and more often. So, I decided to be obedient.

When I was at your Love Life Women's Conference 2012—30th Anniversary last year, an amazing thing happened.

Saturday morning while singing and praising our heavenly father, I was touched. Someone from the row behind me laid their hand on my shoulder. I began to cry. I wasn't sad. But it was as though someone had turned on a faucet. Tears just continued to pour out. It started with slight pressure I could feel pushing down on the palms of my hands, making it difficult to keep them raised. Next, I felt the pressure move to the top of my head. And before I knew it, I was on the ground. It was a graceful falling. I could not get up. The best way to explain it is muscle testing, the method holistic doctors use to test foods that may be sensitive to our system. My body was so heavy I had no control over it. I felt as though I was being held down. I tried to open my mouth to speak, but my jaw was knocked to the left side, and all I could do was drool.

While on the ground, I felt this peace come over me. I saw burdens I had been carrying flash before my eyes. And I heard a voice confirm my desires to help end world hunger. God told me the slogan "enjoy the journey" for our cookie company and told me that he would provide me the people to complete the work. He also told me to get rid of my house. I could hear people around me praising the Lord, saying, "Yes, Lord, yes, Lord, fill her." It did feel as though I was being emptied out and filled up. I started to regain strength and lifted myself back into my chair, all the while shaking and crying and laughing uncontrollably. All the women around me were laying hands on me, telling me that the Holy Spirit had come down and touched me. My friend Ann, who I came to the conference with, was hugging me, telling me over and over how she had prayed for this moment. I then began to hyperventilate, cry, and rock myself in comfort. I was incredibly overwhelmed with emotion. I was elated and frightened. I then reached over to the stranger sitting beside me, who was holding my hand, and put her hand against my cheek for comfort and reassurance of the fact that I indeed was not dreaming or imagining this. Wow. It was incredible. I remember a lady a few seats down telling me how blessed she had been by witnessing what had just happened to me. I felt the need to tell her that I felt as though I had just given birth to myself. The funny thing was I never got an opportunity to actually give birth. My daughter came by way of emergency C-section. She then told me that that was the most powerful description she had ever heard in all her thirty years of being a

Christian. I knew it was God who touched me. But part of me wondered if it really did happen. So, I quickly swung back around and asked the row behind me, "Who touched me?" I repeated it over and over while crying. Finally, someone said, "It was me." I held her hand and said, "Thank you." I repeated it over and over.

I then leaned over to the stranger sitting in the seat to the right of me, kissed her on her cheek, and told her, "Stop beating yourself up. God loves you just the way you are."

She began to cry and thanked me. I did not know why, but I felt the need to tell her that and to kiss her! She told me, "I needed to hear that so badly." Deep down inside, I knew. I don't know how or why, but I did.

Because I wanted to be reminded of this amazing day in my life, I asked for a few people's contact information so I could keep in touch—Emily, the girl who touched me, and Lorrie, the stranger who sat beside me.

After the afternoon service, while I was heading up the stairs to leave the auditorium, I was stopped by random people at different times. They leaned over and tapped me to tell me things. Each one was something different, confirming what I had heard from my time with God. It was unbelievable! I really had to ask myself over and over, *is this really happening*? Good thing I came with my friend Ann and she witnessed it all. She said, "Yes, Monica. It is!" Mind you, these people had not been sitting nearby, and I had not shared with anyone what God spoke to me about. That experience was so impactful. I did as I was moved to by the Holy Spirit.

I came home and shared what had happened with my husband. He did not question it at all. He agreed to put the house up for sale. We began looking into it. In the meantime, we got a phone call from Carrie, a neighbor who had been renting the house across the street. She had heard that at one time we were trying to sell our home. It was true; we had it up for sale a few years back. She thought it may have been our plan still, and if so, she wanted to rent it from us. Perfect. Wow. What timing! I thought it was divine. So, the four of us sat down to discuss the opportunity.

A few days later, Lorrie, the woman I had met at the conference, called asking me how I liked it and what God shared with me while I was down on the floor. I told her everything except for the selling of the house. I felt it was of no need; I already had a buyer, and everything was all set. She then went on to share a personal experience of how God spoke to her several years back, asking her to sell her home. She was going through a divorce and felt it would be best for her children and herself not to be uprooted. However, that plan backfired. She was sobbing. It really was heartbreaking to listen to. She then said, "I don't know why, but I felt the need to share that with you."

"Well" I said, "I know why you felt the need to share that with me. God told me to get rid of our home, and we are. Our neighbors are going to rent it from us." I told her how it felt so divine.

She then firmly said, "God did not tell you to rent it! He told you to get rid of it. To sell it!" I did not want to sell it. We had built our home in 2004 when the market was hot. Having paid top dollar for it, we'd be upside down. That's *ridiculous*! Not to mention all the additional monies we poured into it with the landscaping and other upgrades. After we got off the phone, I started to have second thoughts about renting to my neighbor. I wondered if I was being obedient. I was not physically living there any longer; they would be. However, it would still belong to us. Technically, we were not getting rid of the house. *Did God send Lorrie to call me?* With that thought, I ran over to my neighbor's home and apologized, telling her we changed our mind and would no longer be renting out the home. It had to be sold. They were so taken back by this change of heart. I offered them the option of purchase but again shared that we couldn't rent. I shared the story of God speaking to me and how I got this random call from a woman I met at the conference. That discussion did not go well. Word got around, and soon the entire neighborhood ended up getting involved. They were so upset with us and felt it was hypocritical of us to set Carrie and Tony up like that. It was awful. We had been living in the neighborhood for seven years. Most of us built together and had been there since the beginning. Strong friendships had been made, or so we thought. That was very disheartening. We were willing to sell by owner to them, but since they were not interested in buying but rather wanted to rent, my husband and I sat down and discussed where we needed to be to break even and put the house up for sale on the market. The real estate agent was so amazed we had more than three hundred hits the first day it was up. Mind you, the market was at a terrible low. This was October 2012. Homes were not selling. However, we knew in our hearts this time it was going to sell, and it did. Sold and closed in only fourteen days.

The planner in me would have thought of where to go first, but I was feeling the need to just be obedient. Therefore, we were praying and waiting on God to tell us where to go.

It was drawing close—closing day, and we still did not have a clear direction as to where to go. Then Lorrie called again and said, "If you have nowhere else to go, you can always go back home (to Michigan)."

Funny, my dad had offered us the opportunity to say with him and my stepmother if we needed, in order to give us ample time to get reacquainted with the area; it had been eight years since I had lived there. So, we took them up on the offer, put all our stuff into storage, and moved in. The more I thought about it, the more we realized that Michigan had a much better opportunity for yumbitz. The Detroit area was starving for entrepreneurs. Not to mention my support group of friends and family. They helped me with my first business endeavor, the childcare, Miss Monica's Little Friends, and now yumbitz—cookies on a mission.

The journey lasted longer than expected. It took *seven* months (*felt like forever*) for us to find our home. It was difficult for everyone involved. We almost broke up and lost our relationships with family.

Angel Number 7—Joanne Scribes

Tell of a beneficial time to learn and succeed in self-mastery and self-control, and implies that with enough strength of purpose, ambitions can be realized and obstacles overcome.

WONDERS

Letter to Joyce Meyer Continued

I was so excited to go to the conference. I was packing to get ready for my flight to St. Louis, and I heard *"Chips and socks." Chips* became so loud, I finally went to the cabinet and pulled out a bag of Lays chips and packed them in my carry-on. Once they were secured in the bag, I felt at peace. Then I heard *"Socks. Pack socks."* OK. So, I packed socks.

I arrived at the airport, and the woman who I was sitting next began complaining about her sister and how she had to wake up so early to get to the airport. She was so upset with her for forcing her out of the house in such a rush that she forgot her chips. *Chips?* My ears perked up. I continued to listen. When she was off the phone, I told her to look in my bag. She looked at me with suspicion and confusion. I said, "Look inside my bag." I brought the bag closer to her face. "Do you see what's in there?"

She said, "Yes."

I said, "What do you see?"

She said, "Chips?"

I said, "I brought them for *you*." She looked puzzled. I told her, "I don't even eat chips, and I am headed to the Joyce Meyer Conference. The plane ride will be short, and when I arrive, I'm headed straight to the conference. The chips I brought were for you." I told her about the little voice I heard while packing. She had a big smile on her face.

This year, I attended your women's conference as well. It was amazing how it all worked out. I wanted to go, but all the hotel rooms were booked when I went searching, at least the ones nearby. My stepmom-in-law, Barb, came for a visit and expressed that she had always wanted to see you live. My husband said it would be meant to be if he could find us a room on such short notice. He logged onto the Marriott website, and what do you know—one room became available.

So, we were on the plane headed from Chicago to St. Louis when Barb asked to see the tickets. *Tickets?* (Gulp.) I had no tickets. I had been wrapped up in the joy of having found a room for the conference that I completely forgot to reserve tickets to your show.

Once the plane landed on Thursday night, we did our best to get over to the Dome in a hurry. Lots and lots of people were headed to the same place; it was crazy busy. We managed to fight the crowd and head in to purchase tickets. Your staff was very attentive and ushered us right in. Finally, we were in line to purchase tickets, and one of the staff members took my credit card. When she came back, I was expecting to sign on the dotted line, but she put her hand on my shoulder, looked me in the eye, and said, "God has *big* plans for you! We got it. You owe us nothing." Barb looked puzzled. Neither one of us could believe what we heard. "Thank you?" was all I could say. I was so overwhelmed with emotion. The staff hugged me and told me to enjoy our time.

The show was about to begin in forty-five minutes. The place was packed. Everywhere we walked to, we were told the seats were all taken. I was drawn to the center balcony. I did not want to have to sit way up, and neither did Barb.

I went back to the area I felt called to. I asked the usher if there were any seats available. She said, "Only singles." As I agreed to splitting up, a woman stood up in the aisle and said, "I have been saving these seats for you."

I could not believe it. "For us?"

"Yes! For you. God has big plans for you and wanted you to be here."

"Wow!" This was unbelievable. Barb could not get over the favor and blessing we were receiving. She had to call and tell her husband, Mike. It was pretty incredible! I felt loved and supported.

At break, we decided to go on a tour of the Dream Center. As we were climbing the stairs, Barb was gripping the handrail in an effort to stay upright. She could not stand up or walk. She was forced to her knees. Hanging on the railing, she looked up at me, crying, confessing to me. She spoke of a time in her life where she moved into a place like that to escape her husband. It was one of the hardest things she ever had to do, and she said she made a promise to God that she would be back to tell the women who were going through something similar that it would not always be this way, that it would pass.

CHAPTER 14

FORGIVENESS

> To forgive is to set a prisoner free and
> discover that the prisoner was you.
> —Lewis B. Smedes

When you forgive, you do not change the past, but you do change the future. What I have learned is forgiveness heals all. It is the guiding force that mends our deep wounds—wounds we sometimes do not realize we still carry.

We were on a Disney cruise. I had suddenly awakened from a realistic dream. You all know what I'm talking about, the kind that felt so real that you swore it happened, and it is hard to convince yourself otherwise. Well, that was what I was experiencing. In the dream, my ex-husband and his family were trying to find me. When they did, they were talking to me and hugging me. The crazy thing is I had not heard from them in many years. And there they were in my dream, talking and hugging. It was so real, and I was happy. I really did miss them. I spent most of my teenage years at their home. Almost every day after school, I was there, and on most weekends. I tried not to think more about it, but it just felt so real and so needed. My heart was mourning their loss.

We approached shore later that day, the last day of our cruise. Once we got to land and received cell service again, my Facebook began pinging and notifying me of various messages, one of which was from Katie (my ex-sister-in-law). She sent a message telling me of how Joe wanted to talk with me; she asked if my number was the same and if it was OK for her to give it to him.

Immediately, I flashbacked to the dream I had and wrote back that it was. I have to admit it got me wondering.

A few days later, I got a call from a number I did not recognize. On the other end of the phone was a familiar voice. "Hello? Bean? I'm sorry." Tears just poured down my face. It took a few seconds for me to digest what had just happened. *Was I still dreaming? Was it Joe?* Then I snapped back to reality. It indeed was him. He began apologizing over and over, sharing with me how he had heard about how I was praying for him, and it touched his heart. He felt the need to reach out to me and say sorry for everything and to let me know just how amazing of a wife and friend I truly was and how he did not really know it until he heard how I prayed for him after his fall. You see, back in May 2013, while at a birthday party for my cousin, someone slipped up and shared with me how Joe had had a terrible fall. He, his mom, and son were hiking in Big Sur in Northern California. He went out to get a better view for a picture, slipped on the moss, and fell thirty feet off a cliff and into a rocky ravine. I gasped when I heard. I guess it was all over the news. At the time, I was living in Chicago, so I did not see the report showing how he had been rescued. My heart hurt. Although we were no longer together, I still cared about him and only wanted good for him. I immediately shot a text to his mom. I did not know if it was still her number after all these years, but I wanted her to know I was praying for him. No response. Fast-forward six months to November 4, 2013 (on our wedding date, thirteen years later). I get the call. He thanked me for caring and expressed how it touched him that after all we went through, I said I was praying for him. He began to tell me how his second ex-wife, whom he had a child with, wished he would have died. But me, I was praying. I asked why he called. He told me how he and Selene had been sharing stories about their past relationships. Selene was his girlfriend at the time of the fall. He told her all about his second ex-wife and then about us. When she heard our story, she stopped him and said, "What you shared about Monica ... I think you should reach out to her." She told him that he was the bad guy, that I loved him so much and probably was still holding on to the hurt and that he needed to call and free me. He then said to me, "That is what I am doing. I am calling to apologize. I hope you can find it in your heart to forgive me." I just cried and cried.

All those years, I thought I had moved on and it was no longer a thing for me, but the last few months, something was holding me back from moving forward in life. Something kept coming up—fear of failure. I replayed many events in my mind, checking each one off a list. I was at a loss. *What could it be? What did I fail at?* Then the call. *It was my marriage.* Fear of failure. I felt like a failure because I gave up on my marriage, although in my heart I felt like I did everything to keep it together. But there were so many things I could no longer live with. I knew it was the best thing for me, but *was it? Did I give it my all?* Or did I just give up? I'm not a quitter. I am not a failure. One may even call me an overachiever. Like I said, everything I do I give 100 percent, all my heart and soul, but I was done. I felt at the time it was one-sided. I did not like the way my life was going. I looked at the lives of the women around me who were older than me, living miserably, dealing with their marriages. I did not want that for myself. That phone call freed me. It instantly healed my heart and gave me the confidence to move forward and pursue my dream. I was *not* a failure.

I then began to share with him all that had transpired in the last ten years, all about the jobs I had, and how I started this cookie company I was about to launch, and how I felt something was holding me back. How often I had heard the words *fear of failure* ring in my ears, and now I knew what it was. I was so thankful for his call. That moment forever changed my life. He cried. I cried. It was a powerful conversation, one that was a long time coming. The amazing thing is Joe's a creative director for an advertising firm. He went to school and made a profession out of marketing brands, and here I was with this brand, yumbitz. He took a look at what I had put together and immediately started asking who helped. I told him it was David, me, and God. God gave us the vision, and we just brought it to life. He told me it was great and how impressed he was.

Side note: I joked about how sitting in on his college courses at CCS, Center for Creative Studies, paid off. Fun fact: famous artist Wyland studied there too.

I must have learned a thing or two. We laughed. He told me that if I ever needed any help not to hesitate to reach out. He believed in me and wanted to help in any way he could. Our conversation was incredible. We talked for hours, and he listened. He just listened as I cried and poured my feelings out as I shared the story about my life. Joe was always the dominant figure in our relationship, so this was a big deal. I thanked him over and over and told him how much I already loved Selene and how I felt he was married to Jesus. In all honesty, it was powerful the words he chose. It was as though I was talking with Jesus, not Joe, on the phone. He knew all that I was still broken by. He called it up one by one and freed me. It was amazing! Forgiveness is a beautiful thing. You know, I've always read how God heals broken hearts, and now I know! I've read how he counts and collects our tears in a jar.

> You keep track of all my sorrows. You have collected all my tears in your bottle.
>
> You have recorded each one in your book. — Psalm 56:8 (NLT)

He never forgets. God cares about each and every one of us. We are his beloved children, and now I *know*! He makes our wrongs right.

However, it was only possible with me *choosing* to forgive—not to place blame but rather to hear each other out, to realize that we both had needs and feelings that were not being acknowledged or met. It took two of us to fall apart, and it took two of us to make it whole again. Everything indeed happens for a reason—not to hold on to it but to let it go, to trust it was part of the journey.

Karly had been playing in the kids' club at the gym. She and another little girl, McKayla, happened to both wear pink Crocs. When we went to pick up Karly, we noticed her Crocs were missing. There was a mix-up; McKayla had accidently worn Karly's Crocs home. How did we know that they were not Karly's? Karly's Crocs were worn in—dirty and very comfy. McKayla's Crocs were like new. The caregiver called McKayla's mom and dad and explained the situation. We were asked to wait in front of the building for her parents to bring them back.

"Monica? Is that you?" I heard a familiar voice ask as she walked up to the building.

Shirley? "Yes," I replied.

"I always wondered what happened to you!" she said. I thought, *Funny. You fired me.* Shirley was the owner of a childcare center I used to teach preschool at. I had worked there for five years. I loved my job! I had just bought a home and was thinking of opening up Miss Monica's Little Friends, but I was really happy and comfortable in my role at her facility. Word got out that I was thinking of starting my own in-home daycare, and Shirley was not at all happy. The week after 9/11, I was ushered into the office. She and Debbie, the director, wanted to talk to me in private. They asked me if the rumors were true, and I said that they were. Then they fired me. They told me to drive around to the back to pick up my belongings, as they were waiting for me outside the door to my room, in the alley. I could not believe what was happening. Thirteen years later, here she was!

I began telling her how I had been and about my divorce from Joe. She had been at our wedding. I told her about meeting David and the move to Chicago and the fact that we were back in the Mitten. She was in a hurry and had to get to a class, so she apologized and passed along her phone number. She asked me to reach out to set up a lunch date. I hesitated for a few days but decided to call.

We tried to figure out a day and time that would work, but I could not get a sitter lined up, so I invited her over to my house, and I made us a delicious salad to enjoy. We spent more than three hours together. I told her about yumbitz and the longing on my heart to write a book. I also shared the dream I had about Karly. She then shared her story about a similar situation. She, too, was having a difficult time getting pregnant. She was desperate. A loved one encouraged her to make her request known to God. She flew to Saudi Arabia to light a candle in a place of worship that was very dear to her family, when a gust of wind blew in, knocking her to the ground. She told me it was so strong it literally knocked the wind out of her. The next day, as she was headed back from the adoption agency she had been working with, she received a call; they had a child for her! That same day, she discovered she was pregnant with a child of her own!

We bonded, hugged, and shared tears and smiles. I was happy to have this part of my heart healed. It had been thirteen years. Thirteen years I dreaded. Thirteen years I beat myself up over having been fired.

Now I realize that if I had not been fired, I would not have had the courage to start my own business like I had always dreamed of doing. I remember the whispers, the nudges that I did not take. I just got kicked is all. Miss Monica's Little Friends—I had a whisper on my heart come over me earlier that year. We recently had purchased a home, and I was thinking of ways to open my own in-home daycare. I met with the state and interviewed other people who had their own daycares to better understand the commitment and all that was involved. I did the homework. God was just pushing me to make my move.

Angel Number 13—Joanne Sacred Scribes

Angel number 13 may be a blessing in disguise.

Who Do You Need to Forgive?

Forgiveness is the secret to living a life you love.
Take this time to jot down names of people and offenses.
I dare you to reach out to them. No matter how much time has gone by or how badly they've hurt you—or you them—there is power in forgiveness. Choose to grant yourself the power and grace.

There is power in forgiveness!

Forgiveness does not mean you consent to what transpired; rather, it releases you from the bondage that has occurred as a result.

Forgive yourself.

CHAPTER 15

BLESSINGS COME IN DISGUISE

*Opportunity often comes in disguised in the
form of misfortune, or temporary defeat.*
—Napoleon Hill

Fear of failure played over and over in my mind. It began to infiltrate my decision-making, affecting all areas of my life. I was petrified, constantly wondering if I was making the *right* decision.

We moved back to Detroit (from Chicago), and it hit me hard. I struggled with finding the right house in the right area, and if that wasn't enough, I needed a car. I did not purchase a car for months. We moved back in December, and it took me until August to buy one. I talked myself out of everything. I was worried about how it would fit into everyone's life. I was now living in the Motor City; therefore, I felt the need to purchase a car from one of the Big Three. Plus, my dad worked for GM, and I felt the need to support him. People in the Detroit Metro area were pretty vocal about how they felt regarding foreign vehicles. Some people have been known to yell at you, call you names, spit on your car, or key it!

Then, as for living arrangements, the issue was, how far away from family and friends did I want to live? I really wanted to live on the west side, but everyone I wanted to see lived on the east side. And in the Detroit Metro area, there is a serious divide between the east and west-siders.

I had criteria based on a vision I saw in my head. I was on the hunt for the home that matched that vision—open floor plan yet compartmental, complete with a wall of windows, lots of trees, modern yet unique. It was clear in my mind, but after visiting more than twenty-five homes, I didn't find it. I fell in love with other homes and was outbid, or the homes sold out from underneath us. If you remember, 2013 was a crazy time. Homes were selling for well over asking price, inventory was super scarce, and what was on the market was either in poor condition or had been raided by squatters/thieves who stole plumbing and more. My Realtor, my cousin Michael, was beginning to get extremely frustrated with me. I had hired him, and I'm sure he was wishing he had not agreed—as well as everyone else who was involved, especially my dad and Nancy.

When I finally found the house I wanted, my high school friend Corey, who had been in the real estate business for more than twenty years, told me that he felt that it was a *ridiculous* buy. He expressed his concern with regard to how much work it was going to need. It still had the original windows and doors from the sixties. They were definitely not energy efficient and would need replacing soon. It also had an outdated kitchen and bathrooms, septic tank, baseboard heating—the list went on. But something in my spirit just told me, *this is the one. This is our house.*

People were losing homes to foreclosure and doing whatever they could to get their money's worth. Then we finally found it! Our home! It was complete with windows and trees and an open floor plan yet compartmentalized, just as I had envisioned. It was a gorgeous, custom *Better Homes and Gardens* California ranch.

It had a unique layout and design. We were so excited. Finally, after seven long months, we were going to have a place to call home again. However, this home came with lots of secrets. We thought with a little sprucing up, it would be perfect. But as we prepped the walls for painting, we discovered something. You see, Andy, a friend of mine who just happened to be a master painter, helped us by going from room to room, looking for imperfections. He was preparing walls for paint. In the living room, he noticed under the window there was an air bubble. He began to tap on it with a wall scraper, and that was when the wall shattered. Bits and pieces of dry wall were all over the floor. He continued to pound on the wall, exposing the rotten wood underneath and the black mold that lurked behind the wall. My heart sank, and then fear crept in. *Oh no!* I feared for my family's health and wondered what we had gotten ourselves into. He told me that he could help us remove and rebuild the wall. My cousin was an environmental scientist and had the means to exterminate and treat the infected areas. We found this in a few other areas around the house.

The story goes that the house had had a new roof put on a few years prior to the previous owners moving in. There must have been a leak, and they repaired the roof but did not look into the potential damage that may have resulted from the leak—hence the mold in the wall. I was devastated and shocked. Why was this happening? Why me? Once again, God provided us with the help we needed. He introduced us to Andy and our contractor, Nick, months before we even bought the house. We were visiting my sister, and Nick and his fiancée, Shannon, were there. Shannon was telling us how they were getting married soon and how Nick had started his own company with a friend to do remodels.

As the conversation progressed, I realized why God had brought them to us. Nick and Andy were out of work and needed money to pay their bills; our nightmare was their blessing. We needed them, and they needed us. Funny thing is I asked God for a home that was like new but was old and unique, and I surely got that. We worked on restoring our home for *forty* straight days! By the time it was all said and done, we knew every inch of our home, and many parts were indeed like new. We made out financially as well.

Angel Number 40—Joanne Sacred Scribes

> Angel Number 40 is a message that you are protected, safe and well-loved. Your angels ask that you take a moment to reflect upon this unconditional love, and know that all is happening for your highest good. You have been diligently building solid foundations and the work and effort you have put towards achieving your goals and aspirations will see you reaping your desired results. You have it within you to overcome any obstacles you may encounter along your path.

The moral of the story is don't overthink everything and be careful what you wish for. What I looked at as a failure was a blessing in disguise. Things happen to us or work through us. (Side story: While writing this book, I was prompted to call a friend back in Plainfield, Katie. I was sick with a cold and had just stopped to make myself a cup of tea. A little voice said, *"Call Katie."* I did. I began sharing with her how I was writing my book and how excited I was. She interrupted me and began to tell me how her husband, Bill, remembered something from a fellow church member's testimony that really stuck with him. He said, "Things happen to us or work through us." The crazy thing is I had just finished writing that exact phrase down. Just more confirmation to me that someone was helping me to write this book.)

I have come to learn the very things we fear are what we need to face! On the other side of fear is freedom! Trust the process.

CHAPTER 16

ANGELS AMONG US

> Not all angels reside in heaven. Some
> walk the earth. Just like You!
> —Ask Angels

My dad and stepmother, Nancy, were coming in town for the weekend to visit, so I headed to Meijer to pick up some food for the week. In Meijer, I saw a woman who was mentally disabled. She was motioning me to the deli counter. She reached in her back pocket and pulled out an envelope and began to open it. Inside was a cutout of what appeared to be a snowflake, but upon further examination, it was an angel. I smiled and gave her a thumbs-up.

As I was headed out to my car, I heard a familiar voice from behind me. "Hey, Monica! Monica, how are you? It's me, Cynthia!" I did not want to see her. I was actually very upset and disturbed that I even ran into her. Years ago, I was part of a religious group and chose to leave. Seeing anyone from that organization upset me.

I quickly shut down the conversation and hustled to the car. The cart boy met me at my car. He asked if he could assist me with my bags. I said, "Yes." He began to load them into my trunk one by one. Then he turned to me and said, "Ma'am, you are surrounded by myriads and myriads of angels. Jesus has got your back!"

I looked at his name tag—Alfonzo—and said, "Thank you, Alfonzo! I needed to hear that more than you know."

I did not tell him what was going on in my head. *Why is he saying that to me?* He left. I got into the car and just began to cry. I called my pastor. I shared with him what had just happened, and he said I should go into Meijer and tell the manager how much I appreciated Alfonzo's help. So, I did just that. I jumped out of the car and hurried in to customer service. I asked, "May I speak with the manager?" He came out. "I just wanted to tell you how much I appreciated Alfonzo and all his help—and to tell you what a stellar employee he is."

The manager gave me a blank stare and said, "I'm sorry, but we do not have anyone who works here by that name."

I said, "I saw him. He was in the parking lot. I read his uniform. His name badge said Alfonzo."

"Again, I'm sorry, but we do not have anyone by that name working here."

I could not believe what I was hearing. It was just a few minutes ago. He was there. I saw him. He talked to me. I went back to the area. On the way, I scanned the parking lot, looking everywhere, but he was nowhere to be found. I quickly called the pastor again and explained all that had happened, and he said, "Monica, I believe you had an encounter with an angel."

That was not the first time I had an encounter with an angel.

My stepmom-in-law, Barb and I were waiting outside the Marriott to catch the shuttle for dinner after day one of the Joyce Meyer Women's Conference. Two people approached us, a man and a woman. They were selling newspapers to raise money for the facility they lived in, a halfway house. They appeared to be recovering drug addicts. I met them halfway to learn more about what they were up to.

Barb clung to the wall, clutching her purse close to her body. As I approached, the woman said, "Some of us have forgotten where we came from," looking at Barb.

"People are trying to climb the ladder to heaven, forgetting who's holding the ladder. Jesus," her partner said.

They invited us to come and pray with them. I was all about it, but Barb was very apprehensive. I encouraged her to come over. Finally, she did. We all held hands and began to pray. Then our shuttle arrived, and we parted ways. Once I sat down on the bus, Barb told me that fifty years ago, she lived in a shelter after she left her abusive marriage. During that time, she made a promise to God that if he saw her through it, she'd return to the shelter and help the women there to understand everything will be OK and it won't always be like this. In that moment, seeing those two people, she remembered that she never fulfilled that promise. After she finished telling me her story, I looked for them out the window, and no one was there. They were nowhere to be found! I felt chills and knew those two "people" were angels in disguise, sent to remind Barb of the promise she had made.

CHAPTER 17

KNOWLEDGE AND UNDERSTANDING

> Understanding is deeper than knowledge.
> There are many people who know you, but
> there are few who understand you.
> —Unknown

There comes a time in our lives when we are no longer satisfied with the world and all of its offerings. Nothing will quench our soul—no *body* and no *thing*. There comes a time when we no longer seek to go outside ourselves but rather within. You retract.

For instance, I used to love shopping and decorating my home. It excited me to run into Marshalls, TJ Maxx, or HomeGoods to seek out and bring home the latest treasures, to find that one piece to add to or transform a room.

Whenever I was sad or depressed, I'd find comfort in the hunt. It would bring me happiness to step back and see just how perfect the new piece was. However, I have come to a place in my life where that no longer serves me, along with so many other things that did.

I found myself no longer fitting in with a group of friends or family

I once found joy with. I was on a quest for something more, something I could not quite put into words. It was an inner knowing of something that I could not see but could only feel with my heart, a longing to be made complete and whole. I have known this most of my life. It started to call out to me as a young child. My parents took me to church, and I thought I found it there. I felt comfort and a level of understanding for the world and how I fit into it. But it did not define me and tried to mold me into someone other than who I am. It taught me that I could be someone, but in my heart, I already knew "I am" someone. I am the light of the world, the beacon in the darkness. But it was not until I exhausted all my external resources that I found what I was looking for. It was with me all along.

People repeatedly commented on how I had changed. I immediately tried to search for who I used to be, to find out where and when I lost myself. I felt so misunderstood and rejected, judged and not good enough. I was saddened by the fact that I could no longer relate to or enjoy the things that once brought me pleasure. Nothing seemed to hit the spot, and then the encounters began. Remember me saying sometimes the universe sends random strangers to speak a word to you that just seems to penetrate your soul?

Encounters

At the Joyce Meyer Conference, a woman by the name of Essence was standing in front of me as we stood in line to get our pictures taken. She began asking me where I was from, and then she shared with me how during the entire conference, she had "cookies on a mission" stuck in her head. She told me how it made no sense to her. *It did to me!* Confirmation! I was so overjoyed. We blessed each other. I gave her confirmation about her dream, and she gave me confirmation about my cookies.

Later that year, I met a woman named Sarah when I was sampling yumbitz at the mall kiosk. She told me that she was eating a grapefruit at Panera Bread when the Holy Spirit spoke to her and told her to come down and see me. She came to tell me that I was on the right path and that God had big things in store for me. She asked me what inspired me, and I shared my story. As I spoke, the more excited she became. She told me that, without a doubt, my vision had indeed come from God. She was so moved that she invited me to speak at her church. She then began speaking in tongues over me. I was a little uncomfortable but felt peace with it all at the same time. Everyone who came to buy cookies that day needed prayer or healing or was a Christian confirming the fact I was onto something. It was crazy cool! I realized I am not alone on this journey.

CHAPTER 18

CALIFORNIA DREAMING

> Eventually all the pieces fall into place. Until then,
> laugh at the confusion, live for the moment and
> know that everything happens for a reason.
> —Albert Schweitzer

I'm writing this book as I sit by the Pacific Ocean. Nine years ago, I stepped foot on this very beach for the first time. You see, in 2011, my husband and I had been invited to Orange, California, to meet with our friend Ernie. We were working with his marketing team on some art renderings for crumbz, which later became yumbitz. The plan was to hit up trendy joints for inspiration. After several days of exploration, we were taken to Laguna Beach for some rest and relaxation. As we got closer to the coastline, my heart began to pound. I took in all the sights and sounds. I couldn't quite explain it. It was as though I had been there before.

> Have you ever arrived in a place you've never been before, taken a deep breath & felt like you were home?

Have you ever been somewhere …

I was moved to tears of joy. It felt like home. *How could this be?* It was the first time I ever stepped foot there, yet my soul knew this place. In that moment, I didn't know how, but I knew we were going to live there.

Fast-forward to August 2017. We received a call from Ernie, the same friend who had taken us to the beach years prior. He wanted to run something by my husband, David. Through a chain of amazing events, an opportunity presented itself to fully relocate our family from Detroit to Southern California. He wanted David to be the president of an adult beverage company, a dream of his. This was an opportunity of a lifetime!

Side note: Ernie said he had been meditating at the beach when he heard a voice prompting him to bring the Martins to Orange County. Then this opportunity presented itself. He wasted no time in calling us.

The crazy thing is this was not the first time the opportunity to relocate to California presented itself.

In 2014, my friend Mary and I were talking about how we had heard that Oprah was coming to Detroit. They started promoting the event about a year out. We were determined to go. Appropriately, it was called "Oprah's *The Life You Want* Weekend," and that was exactly what I was working on—a life I love!

> I want us all to fulfill our greatest potential. To find
> our calling and summon the courage to live it.
> —Oprah Winfrey

I really wanted to go, but it was sold out. I was bummed. Shortly thereafter, I received a message on LinkedIn from a recruiter regarding an upcoming job opportunity.

> Brand Ambassadors Needed for TV Hosts National Convention!
>
> Hi Monica, A women's focused inspiration event needs engaging, energetic, upbeat and professional Brand Ambassadors for various roles throughout this exciting 2-day event. Send your resume along with a photo for an interview.

I sent in my resume and photo and was called for an interview.

> Later, I received the following message: "Hi Monica! Congratulations! This is your confirmation for your assignment!"

Amazing! I was given an opportunity to *work* the Oprah event. I thought, *how cool is this! I get to attend the event and get paid for it.* When I arrived for my assignment, I only saw one other vehicle in the parking lot. I thought that was odd. *Where is everyone? Am I at the right place?* I decided to hang out in my car for a while. Then I rolled down my car window to get the attention of the person in the other car. She noticed me. "Hey! Hi! Are you here for the Oprah event?"

She replied, "Yes, I am."

"Where is everyone else?" I asked.

She shook her head and shrugged, responding, "I don't know."

I introduced myself. "Hello, I'm Monica."

She replied, "Hi! I'm Maria." We hit it off right away. Maria happened to live in the next town over from me. We decided to walk over to the assigned area together. We each got assigned different tasks. I was on the bounty team. Maria was on the photography team.

Midday, I received a call from David. He had just been offered an opportunity to move our family to the West Coast. *This is awesome!* "When would they want you to start?"

David said, "Right away!"

When I got off the phone and shared the news with Maria, she smiled and said, "That's cool! I'm moving there myself in a few weeks."

I couldn't believe it. "Really?" I replied. *Wow, that's incredible! Maria will be my first California friend. God is blessing me with her before I even go.* Maria was pursuing an acting and singing career and was moving in with her boyfriend in Altadena. She invited me to bring my family out to California and stay at their place so we could get the lay of the land. So, we took her up on the offer.

There happened to be a home for sale in their neighborhood and an open house. They were offering free tacos and fresh baked cookies. I love tacos and cookies! YUM!(bitz). We decided to check it out. The home was absolutely gorgeous. It had been completely remodeled and listed for $1.9 million. Just a little out of my price range at the time. Sylvia, the real estate agent, was very friendly and hospitable. I began to tell her all about the new job offer and the relocation opportunity. I expressed how nervous I was because I had no idea where to even look. She was so kind and helped me to switch gears from overwhelm to curiosity. She told me that my soul would know where to go. She encouraged me to get in the car, drive around, and ask my spirit what area felt good to my soul. So, I did just that. I got a map of Southern

DO YOU THINK THIS IS ALL THERE REALLY IS?

California and drove from city to city. It took me several days, especially in LA traffic. Once I got on the toll road and headed south, I just kept going. I drove toward Irvine/Tustin, cities that had been recommended to us for our relocation. The homes were beautiful.

Yet after careful consideration and counting the cost, we ultimately turned down the job offer. Why? Because of fear! Although it was somewhere we'd always wanted to live, it just was not right for us financially. We feared being house poor.

When I looked back on it, although I was comfortable financially, I became depressed and had regrets. I wondered, *what would it have looked like if only I had been brave enough to make my move?*

We may feel that we have lost out on an opportunity, but life has a funny way of showing us that if it is meant to be, it will find a way to present itself again. I wonder if this is it the universe's way of asking us, "Just how badly do you want this?"

The three years between the initial offer and the full relocation offer that finally brought us to California for good was filled with so many life-changing events. My father was diagnosed with non-Hodgkin's lymphoma cancer. My teenage niece, Paige, became pregnant and gave birth to my great-nephew, Sammy, and we launched yumbitz. I truly believe that us turning the move down in 2014 was the universe's way of keeping me exactly where I needed to be.

David just got a text from Ernie. He invited him out for an opportunity. Remember I told you about Ernie; he is a marketing professional who had recently partnered with investors to grow his business. The investment group was developing a division of his company with the intent to grow capital investing in small to midsized startups, one of which was a vodka company. It was for the presidential role. David met the group; they fell in love with him and offered him a full relocation package on the spot! It was an amazing opportunity to reinvent himself and double his salary.

Out of nowhere, my friend Katie sent me the podcast "Tired." This podcast was all about recognizing fatigue and exhaustion in your daily life. It was so crazy to me that I had just written about needing rest and relaxation in our lives, and my friend sent me an entire podcast about that exact thing! She had no idea that had been on my heart. I had never shared that with her!

God heard my prayers and saw my effort and knew where I was at. He made a way when I could not. He brought favor and blessings to us. Thank you, Jesus, and thank you, David, for your love and helping to make my dreams come true.

> Journal Entry: August 4, 2017
>
> I have dreamed of this day for so long. Funny, I'm excited about the new opportunity, I look at as an adventure. When I look back on Michigan I am numb. No feelings, I am not sure why. Maybe because it never truly met my expectations. I dreamed of something that was the complete opposite. Friendships are hollow, lacking depth. Relationships with my family feel strained and forced. I did not feel I could just be me.

They say everything happens for a reason. I guess they are right. If I was comfortable and happy there, I would have never ventured out to the West Coast.

CHAPTER 19

RESET

> You were seen, you were heard, you matter.
> —Oprah Winfrey

I promised Karly that I would take her to the pool. The day prior, I got super sunburned, so the splash pad was out of the question for me. Indoor city pool it was. We decided to go and brought her friend Emma with us. We met up with another friend, Rachelle, and her son Andrew.

The kids were having a blast! They had this playscape that had a large bucket attached to it that would fill up and pour water all over the kids. Slides, super soakers, and sprinklers shot water up at them. So fun! There was no way we were getting out of there without getting soaked. Emma and Karly really wanted to try out the lazy river. It had a current that pushed you along, and if you wanted, there were inner tubes available to hold on to or to sit on to enjoy the ride. The only problem was the height limit. Emma passed, but Karly was just below the line. She loved swimming and had been taking classes and felt pretty confident, so we decided to speak with the manager and ask if she could go in. He took her into the deep end to test her abilities, and she passed! Yay! Boy oh boy were they so happy. They were going around and around and around, giggling and smiling. Pretty soon, the pool started to get busy. A group of teenagers came in and began horsing around. They were throwing one another around and dunking one another. I looked for Karly and Emma to encourage them to maybe find somewhere else to play. I saw Emma, but Karly was nowhere to be found. Immediately my heart sank. I shouted out to Emma, "Where is Karly?" She said, "I don't know!" I scanned the lazy river. I did not see her, but I did see an empty inner tube floating by. I looked into the water and saw something blue underneath. "Oh my God! Is that Karly?" I could see that she was struggling to get out from underneath the inner tube. Each time she managed to get up to the surface and lift her head, the inner tube was on top of her, blocking her airway and knocking her back under the water. I was terrified watching her struggle. I screamed at the top of my lungs, "Karly!" Oh my God, Karly! Momma's got you. I am going to help you."

I tried desperately to make my way over to the stairs to get into the river. The stairs were cluttered with moms holding babies and small children. I screamed for the lifeguard to help, but he could not hear me over the roar of the water rushing from the playscape bucket coupled with the children laughing and screaming. I did not know what to do, so I decided to hop over the wall that separated the playscape from the lazy river. As I was running toward the wall, a father of another child saw me and began shouting, "No running allowed!" I did not care. I had to get to my baby girl, and nothing was going to stop me! So, I shouted back to him, "F you! My little girl is drowning!"

As I leapt over the wall, I did not realize the river had several steps leading down into that area of the pool, more than I planned for. Everything seemed to stop, and all I could hear was my heart beat, and my entire body began to tingle from my head down to my toes. I tried to swim over to her, but I couldn't. I had no strength. As I was looking for Karly, I saw the same man who had been yelling at me for running emerge from the water, carrying my Karly. Thank God he saw me and heard me! I was desperately trying to save my daughter's life, and here, a complete stranger did. He brought her over to me. I was crying tears of joy. It was the scariest thing I had ever been through. Come to find out, the reason I had no strength was I had broken my foot on the last step while trying to get to her. I had a metatarsal fracture.

Not too long before Karly's near drowning, I had completed a personal and professional training called Landmark. There I discovered that I do not feel seen or heard, stemming from sexual abuse in my childhood. In the moment that man brought Karly to me, God healed my heart, allowing me to be both seen and heard. I felt like I was being reset.

Thank you!

CHAPTER 20

YOU ARE ENOUGH!

> Sometimes the hardest part of the journey
> is believing you're worth the trip.
> —Glenn Beck

We were celebrating our friend Tommy's fortieth birthday, NASCAR style in Daytona. I was not a fan of Daytona Beach at all. When I was in high school, my boyfriend, Joe, kissed another girl on the pier, and anytime I heard the word Daytona, it made me cringe. After some soul-searching, I realized I left my "I'm enough" there and was determined to use this trip to get it back.

On our way to the pier, we came across two women trying to take selfies. I asked them if they wanted me to take a picture of them. One of them smiled and handed over their camera. They then wanted to return the favor for me and my friends. As we were getting ready, she kept repeating, "Say sex! Say sex!" My Grandma Sarah used to say that every time we'd take family pictures to make us laugh and smile. I was so taken aback I started to tear up and asked her, "Why did you say that?" She began apologizing; she thought I was offended. I was crying because I had just told the story of my quest to get my "I'm enough" back to the bartender. I shared how I had been finding dimes and all about my lovely Grandma Sarah, and then her spirit showed up minutes later through a complete stranger.

We had stopped at the bar to have a few cocktails when I noticed a dime under a barstool. I bent down to pick it up while telling the guy whose chair it was under, "My angel is here!" The bartender seemed intrigued. I looked up at her and began to tell her that the dime was a sign that my Grandma Sarah was with me.

The bartender, Erica, was smiling and replied, "That's awesome!" We got to talking about dimes and signs and the quest I was on. She then told me how she struggled with feeling like she was not enough. Her value was wrapped up in how her parents viewed her and their expectations for her life. For instance, she really wanted to pursue a position in human civil rights, but her parents threatened to disown her for not following their footsteps and becoming a doctor, like her brother. She had no interest in doing so! We encouraged her to do her own thing! We told her that she did not need anyone's approval, that she was enough apart from what she did for a living. We encouraged her to seek out whatever made her soul happy. She thanked us and had to excuse herself because she was crying so hard.

We were off to the pier.

As we were making our way to the pier, there was a woman wearing loud makeup and big hair and carrying a huge wooden cross. She was holding her cross in one arm and was giving out hugs to strangers with the other. With her freshly manicured nails, she passed out tracks. Many people were staring and mocking her as she marched along, piping scripture and telling people, "Jesus loves you!" Although I was not in full agreement with what she had going on, it bothered me to see so many people yelling at her and staring. I commended her for her bravery and love of scripture. She was all smiles. I asked her if we could get a picture together. She replied, "Sure!" We were trying to find someone who was taller than us to take the photo. You know the secret, right? To avoid double chin in a picture, you need someone who can take the photo from above.

I asked several guys on the pier if they would help and was turned down. Finally, we found someone. Wendy, the woman with the cross, seemed to be out of sorts. It appeared that she was on the hunt for something. She'd stand in a spot and say to herself, "No. This is not it. Is this it?" Then she'd move to a different spot and ask herself the same question. I thought she was crazy. Finally, she stopped moving from place to place and said, "Yes! this is it! Right here! This is the spot. Let's take the picture here!" So, I walked over to join her and said, "Cheese!"

Wendy and the wooden cross

When the photo was complete, we took a look at it together. She looked at me as she pointed to the picture and asked, "Do you see yourself? Do you know how beautiful you are? Do you see how amazing you are? Do you know you are enough?" I was so shocked by her stating that and was covered in chills. I was on a quest to get back what I had given away, my power and the feeling of "I'm enough." The moment I found out that my boyfriend had kissed another girl, I told myself a lie and believed it.

With some soul-searching, I realized I had lost a part of myself that day. To some, it may sound silly, even trivial, but to me, it was the end of the world. I remember him coming back from his family vacation—the family vacation I had been invited to but that my parents did not want me to go on. They felt I was too young for all that. I was so mad at my parents and held them personally responsible for what had happened. If I had been allowed to go, it never would have happened. Joe and his family went to Daytona Beach and met up with some family friends. They had a teenage daughter named Brandy, who was the same age as me. The story goes they had met years before while on vacation in Florida, and the families hit it off. They made it a point to get together whenever they were visiting Florida. Joe and Brandy really had a connection; they got along very well and had lots of fun together. I was so jealous of what they shared.

How could I compete with Miss Tennessee? I could not believe that he cheated on me. I was crushed, and in that moment, I felt small and unattractive and told myself I was *not enough*.

While putting the material together for this book, I had to contact everyone who is mentioned in the book, so I was searching for Wendy and came across an article from the *Daytona Beach News-Journal*, "Daytona Woman Bears Cross with LOVE!" by Lacey McLaughlin, April 20, 2014: "Living as a prisoner of addiction and depression for years, Thomas recognizes those who are hurting and longing for redemption and hope."

She redeemed me!

On the way back to the hotel, we spotted a couple sitting in the grass, making palm flowers. Our friend Tommy wanted to stop and watch them, so we joined him. I looked down and could not help but notice what I thought was an "I Am Good Enough" bracelet. The words seemed to shout out at me. I asked her if I could see what her bracelet said, "Oh my God!" I could not believe it.

God really does work in mysterious ways, and the universe is always talking to us and supporting us along the journey, all along the yellow brick road. We just need to tune in!

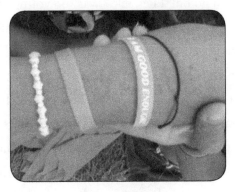

Good Enough bracelet

On the plane ride home, we met Brandon. He was a large man wearing a big gold chain and baseball cap. I offered him a protein bar. I always felt rude eating in front of others. When I was a kid, I was taught if you don't have enough for everyone, then you should hold off. He said he could not. He was watching his weight. It became a conversation about him not feeling like he was enough, and after a few minutes, he began to cry. It was so strange to see him cry. He looked like he could physically take on the world. My heart broke for him. He confessed to me that growing up he had always struggled with his weight, and his parents used to make fun of him for it (His father was a pastor. It seemed weird to me that he grew up in a godly home yet still felt like he was lacking).

He told us that his auntie was the only one who ever bothered to ask him if he was OK. Just then, the stewardess came up to us, looking angry. She turned to him directly and asked, "You OK, boy?" He was sitting with two white people and was crying. I think she may have felt that we were bullying him. But really, our conversation was delivering him from his past. Just like the two ladies on the pier who channeled the words of my Grandma Sarah, it was like the stewardess was channeling the words of Brandon's auntie in that moment. It was like it was meant to be, that we were able to pay forward the amazing gift the strangers on our trip had given to us, the gift of "I'm enough." We ended up exchanging numbers and became friends.

This story reminded me of another time I felt a spirit was talking through another person.

When my aunt Sharon and I baked cookies at the church, oftentimes some of the teachers stopped in to say hello. One of the regulars was Mrs. Tracey. I had not seen her in quite some time. Her mother had recently passed, and she had been in Tennessee visiting family. That day, she popped in to show me a butterfly tattoo she had gotten in honor of her mom. Her mom's name was Shelly. She said she was with her when she took her last breath (what a gift). At that exact moment, her daughter and husband were at the pool, and a yellow butterfly landed on her daughter and would not fly away. My aunt Sharon had just finished sharing a dream she had the night before about her best friend, Shelly, who had passed away earlier that year. I found it cool that she had a dream about her friend Shelly, I had just told her how I felt that Shelly was trying to reach out to her through the dream and it was confirmed by Tracey telling us about her mom. What were the chances? Shelly and Shelly, both with the same spelling, both having passed recently. We were all covered in chills.

CHAPTER 21

ALWAYS HONOR YOUR INNER VOICE

> Listen to your inner voice. Trust your intuition. It's important to have the courage to trust yourself.
> —Dawn Ostroff

It all began with a nagging dry cough. Whenever Karly would talk or sing, she'd have to clear her throat and cough. The cough was persistent and seemed to linger. We tried all sorts of over-the-counter medications and home remedies. Nothing was working. Finally, I made an appointment with the doctor. I am not a big fan of going to the doctor, but I felt we needed some help.

Dr. E came into the room to see Karly, commenting on how good she looked and asking us what we were in for today. I told her about the cough and how it had been bothering Karly for a few weeks. There were no other symptoms. Just the cough. No fever, chills, stomachache, nothing. She was about to send us home, stumped, when she looked in her ears and noticed a little fluid in her left one. Dr. E thought it may be the start of an ear infection and prescribed Amoxicillin.

Upon starting the antibiotic, Karly's cough changed. It became wet, sticky, stringy, and thick. It was difficult for her to cough. It literally choked her, gagged her, and made her vomit. I knew something was very wrong! I called the doctor's office and told them how I thought she was having some sort of an allergic reaction. They said it was not possible; allergic reactions don't cause a cough. They cause a rash. They encouraged me to keep her on the medication and explained that we probably caught the infection early on, and the cough was the way the body was releasing. That did not sit well with me. I had watched her cough change from typical kid cough to this gross disgustingness. My heart told me something was wrong. Those gut feelings you have, don't discount them. They are trying to tell you something.

I began searching the internet for allergies to antibiotics. For hours, I'd search keywords, looking for other stories of people experiencing similar symptoms. Nothing was coming up. A few more days went by, and I called again. This time I was frantic! Again, the doctor reassured me that it was not an allergic reaction and if she was not better by Monday, to bring her back.

The weekend was awful. She was coughing, gagging, and throwing up. Monday could not come soon enough!

Karly begged me to go to school. She hated to miss school and took her responsibilities very seriously. When she woke up Monday morning, her eyes were black and blue and red. She had been coughing so hard in the middle of the night that she popped all the blood vessels. Her eyes appeared to be a pool of blood. She told me it did not hurt, but it looked horrific.

Side note: It was a few days before Halloween. She did not mind it; she thought she looked spooky.

At school, one of her little boyfriends was so concerned that he walked her down to see the school nurse. The nurse gave her an ice pack and asked her a few questions about how she had hurt her eye.

That afternoon, on our way to the doctor's office, she started coughing again. I had to sit in the back seat with her because she would cough and gag and vomit; someone had to be there with a bowl to catch all the yuckies and to help pull out the stringy, sticky mucus.

When we got to the office, Dr. E brought in another doctor, Dr. New, to take a look at Karly. He looked at her eyes, then listened to her lungs and ordered a chest x-ray. After the x-ray, he came back in the room and said that she had pneumonia and we needed to hit this thing head-on! *Pneumonia? What?* I knew she was coughing a lot, but she did not have any other symptoms. My heart just dropped. I was so confused. *How could she have pneumonia when she has no other symptoms?* None of this made sense to me. I told Dr. New that I, too, was starting to get a cough and was scared that I could pass something back to her while she was healing. So, he prescribed me a Z-pack just in case.

My mucus was so thick it was difficult to swallow. I was scared to go to sleep. I'd wake up coughing and gasping for air. It choked me. I started to understand exactly how she ended up vomiting. That was the only way to get it to come up and out. I was terrified to be alone with her. What if I was having a coughing attack when she was? How could I care for her? The round of antibiotics was complete, yet the cough still remained. I called my doctor back in Chicago and an alternative medicine advocate to get their opinions on the situation. They were professionals. Their recommendation was to do another round of antibiotics. I did not feel that was a good idea. She had already had two, and they were not working.

One night, I was so desperate, I pleaded with God. "Please help me! Please, please, please help me to heal my baby girl."

I heard, "Do you believe?"

I replied, "Yes."

I heard, "Then start acting like it!" From that moment on, I spoke life and believed that what I was hearing was truth. "Mold." The little voice inside kept saying, "mold."

> Do you believe? Then start acting like it!
> —God

I had been sharing my frustration with my friend, and she told me about Dr. C, a holistic doctor she took her boys to. I called and left a voice mail requesting an appointment with her. She called me right back. She said she could tell from my voicemail that I was desperate and concerned. She informed that the Santa Ana winds were the worst they'd been in years, coupled with the fires. Bottom line, it was not good air to be breathing in. She also agreed with me that mold might be something that Karly was sensitive to. I expressed to her that the cough came on when she got home after school around three thirty each day. After talking with the teacher, I found out she was only coughing during outside play. Dr. C was pretty convinced it was the air quality and requested that we close all the windows and doors, making our home airtight. She advised us to run the air-conditioning and a vaporizer. She ended the conversation telling me that she was about to board a plane; she and her hubby were headed out of town on a mini vacation and would be returning in a few days. She agreed to see Karly then. In the meantime, she suggested that we see Dr. L, another holistic practitioner. So, we called and made an appointment with her.

We explained to Dr. L the situation from beginning to end. At first, she thought Karly had pertussis. I told her I did not think that was it. I told her I was almost certain the issue was mold. She tested her for pertussis anyway, and it came back negative. She then did muscle testing for bacterial infections. Ding-ding-ding! The results were mold!

The next question was, what was the source of the mold? Was it from the antibiotic, Penicillin, or something else? She wanted us to test the air quality, so we went to Home Depot to get a mold kit. We put it in our living room, and a half hour later, it was covered in spoors! In the directions, it said to send the kit back if there was any evidence of mold; they would tell us what type of mold it was. I did not want to wait on the results. I felt it was time we called in a professional mold inspector.

We decided to contact a local Mold Company. Mike (owner) studied our house for more than three hours. He told us that we should start by getting rid of any of Karly's "made in China" toys. It was like he was mocking the idea that mold from the house could be causing her cough. However, he did as we requested and took more than a dozen tape and air samples.

On the evening of November 17th, Karly was lying on the couch sound asleep when she began to cough. Still asleep, she sat straight up and took a deep breath in an attempt to cough, but she could not catch her breath. All of the veins popped out of her head and neck. It looked as if something was strangling her. I saw her face change from flushed to blue. I shook her and screamed in an effort to wake her up. I was desperate and did not know what to do. I began praying out loud, pleading with God to help! She made the sound of someone who had been drowning and finally regained breath. I just held her. I don't think I fully processed what was happening. David called Dr. C; she told us to get out of the house. She felt it was something in the home that was making her sick. So, we left and tried to find a hotel that would accommodate our family dog, Ruff.

The following day, we received a phone call from Mike, apologizing and urging us to get Karly out of the home immediately! His report came back, and the home tested positive for hazardous levels of Penicillium Aspergillus. This particular mold produces mycotoxins that are toxic to humans if inhaled, eaten, or touched.

The first hotel room had Karly and me in coughing attacks. I sensed this room had more mold than our home. I begged David to move us to another hotel. So, he did; we moved into the Homewood Suites. The room appeared to be much cleaner, and we were breathing easier. Thank God! Upon moving in, our coughing stopped. It's amazing what you take for granted, like breathing.

Mind you, we had just moved into the home three months prior. The last *forty* days of my life had been full of fear, pain, and sleepless nights, not to mention a blow to our bank account—$24,000 in medical bills, food, and housing. It was happening throughout Thanksgiving, Christmas, and the New Year. Karly said, "It was the worst Christmas ever!"

We discovered one of the sources of the mold. An old balcony that had been taken down (twenty-five years old). The wood was dry-rotted and had been stacked in the backyard for more than two weeks during the Santa Ana winds. Having moved from the Midwest, we always kept our windows and doors open to let in the sunlight and fresh air. The mold spores had made their way into our home.

CHAPTER 22

GROUNDED

> You have to keep breaking your heart until it opens.
> —Rumi

I searched for him in people. I went to church to find him. Yet it was not until I went inside that I saw him.

I was so proud of myself for having the courage to step out and do something that scared me. I found reassurance in the fact I had skated in the past and was reminded of the joy it brought me. It had been eighteen years since the last time I put on a pair of roller skates.

Some friends from church invited me out for an open-skate afternoon. I thought it might be fun. So, I took them up on the offer. When I got home, my butt began to hurt. I did not recall falling. It did not make much sense to me that my butt was hurting. I began to feel around to see what might be causing the pain and discomfort. Upon investigation, I discovered a pimple. *A pimple on my butt?* It felt huge. I asked David to take a look at it for me, because that's what you do when your married. He did not want to see my butt under those circumstances. However, he took a look and said, "Yup, you got a pimple on your butt." *Really? Is it possible to have a pimple on your butt?* I went to seek advice. Google of course! Google said it might be a boil.

I had only heard of that word from the scriptures, and it was not a good thing; it was detestable and fearsome.

I needed a professional to help, so David took me to urgent care. The doctor took one look and agreed, "Yes, indeed, you have a boil. We need to lance it in order to release the pressure and allow a healing process to occur." *Really? Lance my butt.* A few minutes later, I found myself lying undressed, facedown, waiting for the nurses to perform the procedure.

Two women entered the room dressed in hazmat suits. You would have thought they were entering a toxic zone. Protection was the utmost necessity from me and my butt. One of them squeezed, and the other assisted with cleanup. When they popped the pimple, the puss shot clear across the room. I heard the one women shriek, "Ewwwwww!" *How embarrassing. I'm still in the room.* They then bandaged me and sent me home with a list of care instructions: be sure to soak for thirty to forty-five minutes each day for two weeks to ensure no infection develops. *You've got to be kidding! Ain't nobody got time for that!*

Oh yeah, wasn't it I who had been complaining about time? I did not seem to have enough, and then *bam*—that. You ask, and you shall receive. What was I going to do? Read. *Yes! You are going to read.* Read what? *Read a book to help you understand that which you don't understand. This Godhead, three in one, the Holy Trinity.* So off to Barnes and Noble I went. I shared with the librarian what I was after, and she directed me to a section, and a book title seemed to yell at me from the shelf. "Read me! This one!" It was *The Forgotten God* by Francis Chan. So, I chose it and read it daily as I soaked in the tub. Grounded. Literally.

That book had a profound effect on me. I began to tell everyone about the power of the Holy Spirit and how we all have this gift available. We just needed to open ourselves up to it.

I became obsessed with understanding this Holy Spirit. What was it? Who was he? What role did he play in my life? Who was this Jesus? Who was God? And what was this gift? It lit a fire in my soul. The God of the universe lives inside you? This is the human spirit.

Signs, visions, wonders, and dreams—the universe is always communicating with us. God lives in us and all around us. Our breath is the gift of life—and promise and proof that we are never alone. You did not ask for breath, and you cannot buy it; it is freely given. A gift. Follow your breath; it knows the way to go. Take deep breaths and allow your lungs to fill with air. Slowly exhale and repeat. Take deep breaths, breathing in all you are thankful for and exhaling all the feelings that bring you down. Breathe in love, joy, happiness, friendship, and fun. Breathe out disappointment, hurt, anger, and feelings of "I'm not enough." Continue this process of breathing in all the good and exhaling all the feelings that weigh you down. Release them.

CHAPTER 23

DREAMS DO COME TRUE

You'll see it when you believe it.
—Dr. Wayne Dyer

I decided to go for it! To make my dreams come true! On September 28, 2020, Balboa Press reached out to see if I was still interested in moving forward with my book. I had reached out to Balboa regarding how to self-publish three years prior. It was the four-year anniversary of my Grandma Sarah's death. I took it as a sign!

-----Original Message-----
From: Monica Martin [mailto:yumbitz@gmail.com]
Sent: Monday, September 28, 2020 7:12 PM
To: >Brian
Subject: Re: Hi Monica, Can we set up an appointment?

Brian,
I would love to discuss this opportunity in further detail. Please let me know a good time to talk.
Thank you, Monica

The following day, I spoke with Brian, and we had one of the most amazing conversations. I began to tell him all about the calling on my life that I could no longer ignore. He told me how he was covered in chills. So was I! I felt supported by God, as if it was he who was leading and guiding me. I had to share this excitement with someone! So, I started with my dad.

Text to my dad: "Grandma Sarah came for a visit last night. She had me look up and listen to these words:

"Somewhere over the Rainbow" by IZ

Oh, somewhere over the rainbow way up
high and the dream that you dare to
So why oh I can't I
And the dreams that you dreamed of once in a lullaby
And the dreams that you dream of
dreams really do come true
And the dreams that you dare to
Oh why Oh why can't I?

The rainbow was a symbol of the promises of the covenant. I also spoke with Balboa Press, and they are interested in partnering for the completion of my book."

Dad: "You know I think my mom came to Nancy and me on the way from up north about seven o'clock. A large rainbow went across the sky. We both looked out the window and just said, "That's Mom." That is a great opportunity that a company likes your story. Congrats to you. Good luck. We love you."

I wrote back, "Think of how cool! You saw a rainbow, and I was prompted to look up 'Somewhere over the Rainbow.' The song is also the vision for the yumbitz candy shop. We got our resellers license today!"

"Very nice. What is a resellers license?" he asked.

"It allows me to purchase products at wholesale for resale," I responded.

He then asked, "What is Balboa? Do you have to pay for this book publishing?"

I responded, "Yes," and told him what the agreement entailed.

He texted back, "OK. Just be careful." He also sent a long list of not so great reviews.

For some reason, those words, "Just be careful," planted seeds of doubt, and I began to question my inner voice. Although I got chills, I began questioning if I was making the right decision. *Be careful* rang in my ear. I was so upset. I did not know what to do or who to trust. I became very rigid and defensive. I immediately sent the nasty reviews to Brian and expressed my concerns. He did a very good job refuting those reviews and helped me to better understand the process. He also reminded me to honor my inner voice, for it knows the way. I decided to sleep on it and told myself, *if by Friday I am still feeling like this is a good idea, I will commit.*

On October 16, 2020 I finally decided to take the leap and go for it! I chose to take the first step in making my dreams come true by partnering with Balboa Press. I felt that the universe was backing me up on this decision by showing me a Facebook time hop from 2016.

October 16, 2016 was the day I was introduced to Jen and Ginger.

Headlines read: "Socially Conscious Artisans, Music Mix at the Mercantile."

It was the first of its kind. Matthew created the event as a way to celebrate the incredible things socially conscious brands are doing, and help bring awareness to the good that is happening; yumbitz was one of twenty-five brands featured. They expected to have more than fifteen hundred people in attendance for this ticketed event. The event would start in Detroit, then to Nashville, and then Los Angeles.

"This is why I am here," my husband overheard a woman say to her friend, as she made her way over to our booth. "There she is!" She was looking right at me. The two ladies approached us and began asking lots of questions about our company—what we were all about and what had inspired us. I shared the traditional response, and then she asked if that was *all* that had inspired me. I replied, "No, there is another reason." Then I began telling her about how I was slain in the spirit at the Joyce Meyer Conference, when the Lord spoke to me and gave me the vision for the cookie company, yumbitz. She then turned to her friend and said, "It is her!"

They introduced themselves. "I'm Jen, and this is Ginger." Jen began sharing with David and I how she had picked up the *Detroit News* earlier that morning and felt led to go to the event. She was not sure why, but she had to go! She called and asked Ginger to join her. When they arrived, she stood in line and felt that she would *know* why she was there once she got inside. And then she saw me.

"You are writing a book?"

What? How did she know? "Yes?" I replied.

"But you are having a difficult time coming up with the title and how to organize the chapters."

I replied, "Yes."

She said, "The Lord sent us to help." I was covered in chills, and my eyes began to well up with tears. *What? This is crazy.* Then Jen talked about how Ginger had been instrumental in helping many others make their books happen and would be willing to assist me in the process. I was so shaken from that encounter. I just began to cry. Wow! *How did they know?*

Two women I had never seen before came to tell me about how they had been sent by the Lord to help me. *Ridiculous* and unbelievable! I asked if we could take a picture together because I wanted to remember the moment forever and have proof that it happened.

Jen and Ginger with David

To be honest, her reply spooked me. However, it did pique my curiosity. So, I decided to meet with Ginger.

When I arrived at her home, I was invited in. It was quite unusual. As we made our way to the table I took note of the curio cabinets and shelves full of inspirational figures—angels, birds, Buddha, crosses, and other spiritual stuff. She offered me a seat, which, I graciously accepted.

Looking through the material I had brought along with me, I started sharing my stories with her. When I told her about the trip to Mexico, she helped me see I already had the title for my book: "Do you think this is all there really is?" She told me the chapters would be the lessons I learned along the journey. I was so happy to finally have direction! I'm not sure why but I got a tickle in my throat and when

I went to try and clear it, I started to cough. I was embarrassed. She offered me a cup of tea; "Green tea please, with honey."

Louise Hay says in her book, "You Can Heal Your Life" that coughing is the body's way of expressing one self- Desire to bark at the world. "Listen to me." Once again, the universe was sending me a sign.

So, I got busy and began organizing the stories. I was so excited and found myself recalling past experiences and encounters with God. The memories began flooding in. I tried my best to capture them, but I got off track, and seeds of doubt started growing again. I was feeling extremely uncomfortable; it brought up religious bondage. Although I was happy to be working with Ginger, I was distracted by the religious idols throughout her home, and I began to question which spirit was leading me. In previous religious groups I belonged to, listening to your inner voice was not a good idea. I was taught to focus on the scriptures rather than my intuition. However, I could no longer ignore the call. My intuition was calling out to me to pay attention, to listen to it.

From Albert Einstein to Steve Jobs, countless thinkers, artists, and inventors have acknowledged their intuition.

Learn to follow your inner voice.

> Don't let the noise of others opinions
> drown out your own inner voice.
> —Steve Jobs

To rediscover your intuition like Steve Jobs did, you first have to get over feeling crazy, different and like you don't belong.

Did you know that detectives have solved countless cases based on hunches? The US military uses their Spidey sense when they need to act quickly.

It is like our antenna picks up universal transmissions and tunes in to our sixth sense.

DO YOU THINK THIS IS ALL THERE REALLY IS?

Time magazine, April 3, 2017:

The US Military Believes People Have a Sixth Sense

In 2014, the office of Naval Research embarked on a four-year, $3.85 million research program to explore the phenomena it calls premonition and intuition, or Spidey sense, for sailors and marines.

Forbes:

Intuition is the Highest Form of Intelligence (February 21, 2017)

The smartest people among us, the ones who make great intellectual leaps forward, have not been able to do so without harnessing the power of intuition.

Albert Einstein acted upon a flash of intuition. He had a notion, one he later called the happiest thought of his life, which led to the birth of the famous theory of general relativity. Einstein concluded that intuition was crucial to the discovery of natural laws.

In 1893, a clerk for a coal company in Detroit came across a contraption made of spare parts and bicycle wheels clattering down the street. He suddenly had a hunch—a flash of intuition. He somehow just *knew* that it was an invention with a future. He immediately withdrew his life's savings of a thousand dollars and bought into the inventor's company. He chose to ignore the experts who insisted that this would never be popular and trust in his own intuition. About thirty years later, he sold his shares in Henry Ford's automobile company for $35 million. To say the least, his intuition paid off!

Keep in-mind that experts and professionals get their knowledge from somewhere… it all started with someone acknowledging their intuition.

Where does their intuition come from? Source- the source of all.

October 16, 2009, was also Boss's Day, the day I trusted my intuition and made my move! I took the leap of faith, put him first, and he blessed me with a baby girl named Karly, just as promised. With the Great Recession, it was *ridiculous* to leave a job, but I chose to trust that little voice inside, to believe the dream, to see the signs and the wonders and follow the visions. I reaped the rewards.

October 16, 2017, was the day we sold our Michigan home, which I was advised was a *ridiculous* buy. However, many were blessed through the process, and we reaped rewards financially.

The date *October 16* has repeated in my life in multiple ways:

- **Sign**- The day I signed on the dotted line and agreed to the terms in the contract to work with Balboa Press to get this book out to you.
- **Dream**- Boss's Day, as asked by God, I put in my two-week notice, and he answered by blessing me with Karly a year and a half later.
- **Wonder**- When I was at the Mercantile event with yumbitz and met Jen and Ginger (earth angels).
- **Vision**- The day we sold our Michigan home, which I had seen in a vision.

Angel Number 16

Number 16 resonates with personal willpower, independence, initiative, action and overcoming obstacles.

> Have the courage to follow your heart and intuition.
> They somehow already know what you truly
> want to become. Everything else is secondary.
> —Steve Jobs

Let's see where God takes me! It's exciting to have witnessed his track record and to have seen his promises come true.

The year I began to listen to my intuition, fame, fortune, and beauty—which were all the things I wanted—died. *All proved to be illusions.*

Fame
Michael Jackson "King of Pop" (June 25, 2009)
Fortune
Ed McMahon (June 23, 2009)
Beauty
Farrah Faucet "America's Sweetheart" (June 25, 2009)

However, having followed the call on my heart, God has taught me to tune in and live in the moment.

"This Moment" by Jeremy Camp

> Singing oh Lord, keep me in the moment
> Help me live with my eyes wide open
> 'Cause I don't wanna miss what you have
> for me (what you have for me)
> Singing oh Lord, show me what matters
> Throw away what I'm chasing after
> 'Cause I don't wanna miss what you have
> for me (what you have for me)

Throughout this book, I have shared personal experiences that have led me to believe in myself, to follow through with the hopes and dreams that have been placed on my heart. I realized that I have been on a quest for something that I discovered was within me all along. Home. A *knowing*. I was on a quest to find true love overflowing, a place where everything has meaning and time is my friend. It is a world that may be perceived as fantasy, but it has taught me love, and it is real to me.

After being prompted to look up the lyrics to "Somewhere over the Rainbow," I could not help but think about Dorthy's quest to seek the Wizard of Oz, thinking he could help her get home. But the power was always her own.

> You've always had the power my dear,
> you just had to learn it for yourself.
> —Glinda, *The Wizard of Oz*

Glinda also tells her that she did not reveal this to Dorothy earlier because she would not have believed it. She had to learn it for herself—to *know* it! Dorothy's journey can be compared to the journey that many of us take, trying to find some "thing" to fill our hearts and make us feel at home. Through the process, we learn that we already had the only friend we ever needed, who promised to never leave or forsake us. We all have this access through the power of the Holy Spirit, the one who promised to always guide us, a.k.a. our intuition. Our intuition is a gift that we must choose to open. May you always *know* you can always come home.

On that day you will realize that I am in my Father, and you are in me, and I am in you.
—John 14:20 NIV

I believe in you!

To be continued …

My hope:

Remember (who *you* are)

CPSIA information can be obtained
at www.ICGtesting.com
Printed in the USA
LVHW041235160621
690357LV00003B/209